## DATE DUE

| | |
|---|---|
| MAR 1 5 '92 | |
| MAY 2 9 '92 | |
| 08 92 | |
| DEC 0 8 '92 | NOV 1 4 1995 |
| MAY 0 7 93 | |
| JUN 0 4 1993 | |
| 11-4-93 | |
| MAR 2 2 '94 | |
| FEB 1 1994 | |
| FEB 2 7 1995 | |
| JUN 1 2 '95 | |
| | |
| | |

BRODART, INC.                    Cat. No. 23-221

# COMMUNICATION CRISIS AT
# KENT STATE

# COMMUNICATION CRISIS AT KENT STATE

## A CASE STUDY

PHILLIP K. TOMPKINS

ELAINE VANDEN BOUT ANDERSON

KENT STATE UNIVERSITY

GORDON AND BREACH, Science Publishers

New York · London · Paris

Copyright © 1971 by GORDON AND BREACH,
                    Science Publishers, Inc.
                    440 Park Avenue South,
                    New York, N.Y. 10016

Editorial office for the United Kingdom

                    GORDON AND BREACH,
                    Science Publishers Ltd.
                    12 Bloomsbury Way
                    London W.C.1

Editorial office for France

                    GORDON & BREACH
                    7-9 rue Emile Dubois
                    Paris 14$^e$

Library of Congress Catalog Card Number: 77-161215

ISBN 0 677 03970 0 (cloth); 0 677 03975 1 (paper).

Printed in the United States of America.

# TABLE OF CONTENTS

# ACKNOWLEDGMENTS

To our colleagues and students who helped with the
interviews:

Ross Andrusko
Mark Cramer
Geneva Damron
Rex Damron
Gayle Epstein
Ray Falcione
Linda Ferraro
Jackie Gant
Betty Gibb
Robin Grimmett
Dominic Infante
Linda Kerns
Judie LaForme
Bruce Landis
Lauren Maser
Linda Moore
Marty Osborne
Mary Lee Rybar
Carol Schlick
Bob Schlick
Charles Waugh
Charles Wrenn

To President White for financial assistance; to Bill
Osborne for advice on sampling; to Ray Bye for innumerable
acts of cooperation; to Judie LaForme for her singular
reliability; to John P. Filo for his photographs; and most
of all to Mrs. Terry Byers for her efficiency and dedication
in arranging interviews, in bookkeeping and in typing this
book.

# COMMUNICATION CRISIS AT KENT STATE:  A CASE STUDY

## Phillip K. Tompkins and Elaine Vanden Bout Anderson

## Kent State University

*Introduction.*  On May 4, 1970, shots fired by the Ohio
National Guard at Kent State University were heard round the
world.  To some they signaled a new war, a second front for
the Nixon administration.  Young people were outraged by the
killings; campus after campus closed across the country in
the days that followed.  The Russian poet, Yevtushenko, wrote
a poem in memory of one of the slain students.  Townspeople,
on the other hand, were outraged by the students.  The old
scar known as the Town-Gown split tore apart--exposing a deep
and ugly cleavage.  "They should have shot forty," some were
reported to say.  Or four hundred.  Or even four thousand.
Kent State University will never again be the obscure university
of Northeastern Ohio.  It will be confused less often with
Penn State in the future.  It has lent its name to symbols
and slogans.

Instant experts rendered the judgment that it was all a
"problem of communication."  We were prepared to test that
hypothesis.  Soon after the tragedies, the senior author
began to conduct in-depth interviews in the manner developed
during his two summers as a Faculty Research Consultant in

Communication at NASA's Marshall Space Flight Center in
Huntsville, Alabama.  He began at the top of the organization
and fanned down and out, listening to the administration
describe what had happened, what problems in communication
they had experienced.

President Robert I. White established on May 21, a
University Commission to Implement a Commitment to Non-Violenc
The senior author was appointed to the Commission and designated as the Chairman of its Task Force on Communication.
(Meanwhile, the authors constructed a standardized interview
guide, revised it six times on the basis of pilot interviews,
selected samples of faculty (153) and students (300) and then
trained a team of interviewers) (chiefly from the faculty and
students of the Division of Rhetoric and Communication.)

As the interviewing progressed through virtually the
entire population of Vice Presidents, deans and department
chairmen the sample was increased by the "snowball" technique.
It became obvious that interviews were necessary outside the
university with the city administration and county officials.
In addition, people within the university who were often
listed as a source of critical information were added to the
sample.

Circumstances were such that this study could not be so
neat as we would have liked.  As teachers we had to complete
the remaining four weeks of the term by meeting with students
in our homes, by correspondence and by whatever other means
we could find.  Drawing the sample of 300 students was also
extremely difficult.  Because the computers were working over-
time with dormitory rent refunds, grades, etc., we drew our

sample by hand--taking every Nth name from the student directory.  The directory had been prepared in the fall and we
found that many of our subjects had been graduated, or had
dropped out, before spring quarter.  In these cases we selected
the name following it in the directory.

Our troubles were not over.  Many of the students had
scattered all over the world.  Those we could locate we interviewed in various ways.  Interviewers living in Cleveland,
Akron, Canton and other cities of Northern Ohio interviewed
many students at home.  Others drove from Kent to Cleveland,
Warren and other cities.  Many interviews were conducted via
telephones.  But still there were some who refused to be
interviewed; a few gave reasons which included fears that we
either represented the FBI or would turn our findings--
including the names of subjects--over to various law enforcement agencies.  In some cases, parents refused to let their
children talk to us.  The saddest reasons, however, for failing to complete interviews were given by parents whose
daughter had been hospitalized for a breakdown, or by those
parents who had not seen their son for weeks, and who had no
idea of his whereabouts.  We feel fortunate to have found as
many as we did.

A further complication was that we felt an obligation to
share our findings with others.  We presented partial findings
and recommendations informally from time to time to people
responsible for emergency operations and communication.  In
addition, from time to time we offered formal recommendations
through the Commission.  For example, it was clear to us by
early June that the communication interfaces between city and

university administrations had completely ruptured (if, indeed
they could be said to have existed at the time of the crisis).
Therefore, on June 15 we offered a recommendation (included
in the appendix) by which to improve the situation.  Other
recommendations based upon partial analysis of our data are
also included in the appendix.

We did not set out to write a history of those days in
May, but the discussion of our data on crisis communication
would make little sense if not placed in context.  The authors
of the definitive account will have to have access to the
FBI report, the Ohio Highway Patrol report and various
commission reports as well as, no doubt, future court trials.
Nonetheless, our interviews involved many participants in,
and eyewitnesses of, the events.  Therefore, we have written
a narrative of our understanding of the incidents of early
May.

We promised confidentiality and anonymity to all subjects
and we have kept our promise in all but one case.  In that
exception, we found that our analysis and narrative of the
crisis period would have been awkward without the permission
to use information given to us by a university official.  The
permission was given.

Otherwise, our narrative follows that given by the
Scranton Commission Report.  We have deviated from that
narrative where our information was different and added to
it when our information was more complete.

We have been extremely critical of the President and, to
a lesser extent, of the higher administration of Kent State
University.  In fact, we have directed some criticism toward

practically all of the principals. but an inordinate amount may be seen to be aimed at the chief administrator. We wish to correct this impression by noting several factors. First, in the same breath by which most interviewees expressed dissatisfaction with the President's communication behavior, they also expressed their profound *respect* for the man. A quantitative manifestation of this may be found in his high credibility rating to be presented later. Ironically, some large part of his failures may well have been caused by his previous successes. From the point at which Robert I. White assumed the presidency to the present, Kent State University experienced a rapid increase in size. We are only beginning to understand the dangers of growth and size.

For example, the Special Committee on Campus Tensions reported:

> *In general, the larger the institution, the more likely it will experience violent or disruptive protest.* Very few institutions with enrollments under 1,000 had any incidents of violent protest in 1968-69. Among institutions of intermediate size (enrollments between 1,000 and 5,000 students), 4 percent of the two-year colleges, 5 percent of the four-year colleges, and 14 percent of the universities experienced violent protests. Of the large institutions (enrollment over 5,000), 16 percent of junior colleges, 14 percent of the senior colleges, and 22 percent of the universities experienced violent protests. There are also correlations with size when nonviolent disruptive incidents are considered.[1]

Perhaps even more dramatic evidence was presented by Harold L. Hodgkinson:

Institutions Reporting Increased Student Demonstrations, by Size of Student Body[2]

| Enrollment | Percent |
|---|---|
| Small--under 1,000 | 14 |
| Medium--1,000-5,000 | 32 |
| Large--5,000-15,000 | 58 |
| Giant--15,000-24,000 | 75 |
| Super--Over 25,000 | 88 |

President White, then, may have inadvertently created some of his own problems by his aggressive leadership during the years of growth. Under his administration, Kent State University became one of the two dozen largest universities in the country.

What may have been effective means of communication and administration for a campus of 12,000 are not necessarily effective for 21,000. Certainly even the mathematical possibilities of communication breakdowns are multiplied during a period of high growth. How many of these additional students came to the university to avoid being drafted to fight in a war they find reprehensible? President White did not start the war, nor did he order the Cambodian invasion--both of which, as we shall see, figured prominently in the Kent State tragedy.

Not all the problems of KSU were reducible to problems of communication. We have tried to avoid the fallacy of the "If-you-don't-do-as-I-demand-then-we-have-a-communication-breakdown!" point of view. KSU clearly faced serious problems other than communication: incompetency, for example, seemed at times to be rampant. Rather, we tried to understand the university from a "systems" point of view, asking whether or not information flowed freely to decision centers and back to action centers for implementation. We searched for isolated subsystems, and defined the most and least credible sources within the university. We found dysfunctions, dysfunctions so serious that they threatened the very operation of the university.

Even though we call this a case study, we think it is

important for reasons other than the fact that it was at Kent State where four students were killed and nine others were wounded. Perhaps there are other universities which have failed to anticipate and prepare for crises we have experienced; perhaps some of our recommendations will be of value in averting further tragedies. More than two-thirds of the nearly 7,000,000 college students enrolled in the fall of 1969 were attending publicly supported institutions--such as Kent State University. Kent State University fell into the "Giant" category of universities--seventy-five percent of which have reported demonstrations. There is a further reason for the possible extrapolation of our findings. There is a large number of former teacher's colleges and "Normal Schools" in our country, like Kent State, who have recently been accorded university status. Again like Kent State, these universities in New York, Ohio, Michigan, Indiana, Illinois and Wisconsin and other states have experienced high growth rates in the past five to ten years. We wish not so much to explain as to illustrate an age.

Finally, we wish to add to the understanding of the problems of communication in large organizations, particularly the university. We should like to caution taxpayers and legislators who might be tempted to effect vindictive legislation, that universities have a unique communication function to perform. What other institution exists for the purpose of seeking and publishing the truth without even editorial restraints? President Nixon said in a televised press conference that this nation will not experience a revolution because we have enough safety valves. He did not add, as we

would have liked, that universities and colleges are among
the most important of those safety valves.  When IBM or the
Bank of America suffer from bombings and fires, public
sympathies are with the institution attacked.  The reaction
is exactly the opposite when colleges and universities
experience the same attacks.  We ought to deplore them in any
case and prevent their recurrence.  But we must not do so in
ways which destroy the unique communicative functions of a
university, for a faulty safety valve has serious dysfunctions
for the larger body it serves.  Or to mix metaphors, we should
consider Clark Kerr's analogy between universities and the
canaries miners took down into the mines to detect by death
bad air.  If the universities die, who will be next?

### *References*

1.  *Campus Tensions: Analysis and Recommendations* (Report of the Special
    Committee on Campus Tensions, Washington, D. C., 1970), p. 10.

2.  Harold L. Hodgkinson, "The Next Decade," *The Research Reporter* (The
    Center for Research and Development in Higher Education, Berkeley),
    Vol. V, 1970, p. 7.

# CHAPTER ONE: THE CRISES, MAY 1-4

The classic Japanese film, *Rashomon*, is the tale of a rape told in different ways by four different witnesses. It is an excellent illustration of the complexities of perception and communication. The rape of Kent State was told to us by almost 500 people, each of whom was involved in some part of the crises.

Certain incidents of this period were described to us in very different ways. In some cases, even the President's Commission on Campus Unrest (the Scranton Commission), with its large staff and access to FBI evidence could not determine which of several contradictory accounts is accurate.

We shall try to unravel some of these knots, but it does seem symptomatic of the many and massive communication break-downs suffered during the crisis that a television series-- "The Bold Ones"--could present a thinly disguised dramatization of these events by means of the *Rashomon* technique.

There is little in the brief history of Kent State University to suggest that its name would become a world-wide symbol. By coincidence, the university was created in the month of May: on May 10, 1910, the Ohio General Assembly passed an act--signed nine days later into law by Governor Judson Harmon--which created what are now called Kent State and Bowling Green State Universities.[1]

There was no Town-Gown Split in those days. The Kent

I

Board of Trade established a Normal School Fund to raise money for the purchase of properties and the paving of roads necessary to the functioning of the school.  Of the 4,488 citizens of Kent in 1910, 563 subscribed to the fund.  Indeed, the citizens of Kent aggressively fought to have the university established in their village rather than in other competing communities.

The first President of the university, John E. McGilvrey, was an energetic disciple of Emerson who could be seen about the small campus planting ivy and pruning plants.  His major innovations were to establish university branches in surrounding communities and a "Pass-Fail" grading system.  He incurred the long-lived enmity of Ohio State University by insisting that the Normal School should not be limited to a two-year course for the training of teachers and by his aggressive campaign for expansion.  McGilvrey was fired on January 16, 1926, by the Board of Trustees for "an unpardonable affront and violation of all customs, ethics and responsibilities of state officials."[2]  McGilvrey had left for Europe on university business on December 14, without asking permission of the Board, leaving the university "without either a president or acting president."[3]

After a long series of upheavals in 1926 and 1927--including the purging of "disloyal" faculty and the censorship of student publications--a student boycott reduced enrollment by one-fourth in the fall of 1927.

Enrollment increased steadily, however, during the Depression--from 679 in 1928 to 2,008 in 1937.  The college became Kent State University by act of the General Assembly in 1935, again in the month of May.

In 1933, the noted lecturer, Dorothy Fuldheim, shocked the faculty and students by predicting war in Europe.  One year later she returned to campus to proclaim that European liberty was prostrate at the feet of resurgent German militarism.  (Now a television commentator in Cleveland, Miss Fuldheim delivered a controversial editorial in May of 1970 expressing her outrage at the actions of the Ohio National Guard in the killings at Kent State.)  During the following year, 1935, 1,200 students "noisily paraded across the Kent campus under a sea of banners proclaiming 'No More War.'"[4] Considering that the enrollment that year was only 1,538, this was probably the highest percentage of Kent State students ever to participate in an anti-war demonstration.

In the spring of 1933, the community and the university were outraged by a report issued by the Finance Committee of the Ohio House of Representatives.  Observing that the state's public schools were saturated with teachers, the report contrasted that fact with the shocking conditions of the state's overcrowded mental hospitals.  Its conclusion:  one of the state's four teacher training institutions (Kent, Bowling Green, Miami or Ohio University) should be transformed into a hospital for the mentally ill.  On that fateful day of Kent's fateful month, *May 4, 1933,* the eight man committee visited Kent to inspect the school.  The entire community mobilized to oppose this proposal, which one area newspaper called "imbecilic."[5]  The proposal was defeated, but there were critics of the university who would argue in the spring of 1970 that the transformation had been accomplished without the benefit of legislation.

From 1938 to 1943, the university was led by President Karl C. Leebrick. Leebrick cultivated the liberal arts, determined as he was to relegate the dominating College of Education to a subordinate role in the university. Leebrick was fired in 1943.

In 1944, the Trustees announced the appointment of Youngstown's Superintendent of Schools, George A. Bowman, as President. As was typical of most universities, the return of G.I.'s jumped enrollments from about 1300 in 1945 to over 6,000 in 1949. ROTC classes became part of the curriculum in 1947. Several "temporary" buildings were bought from army surplus during this period, one of which was used for ROTC classes. "Long years and many coats of paint later," wrote Historian Schriver in 1960, "most of the 'temporaries' would still be in use, the butt of endless jokes on the part of scornful students and instructors alike who knew them all too well as the 'sheepsheds.' Some wondered whether they would still be around to celebrate the University's centennial in 2010. Only time, tempests and termites could tell."[6] Or arsonists.

In August of 1946, Robert I. White became Dean of the College of Education. He had spent the preceding eight years as principal of the high school and president of the associated junior college in Burlington, Iowa. Twelve years later, in 1958, White was promoted to the newly-created position of Vice-President for Academic Affairs. Five years later, he re- placed Bowman as President. The enrollment of KSU under White' administration increased: from roughly 12,000 students

in 1963 to 21,000 in 1970.  Meanwhile, the ratio of Kent
citizens to KSU students had been declining.  While in 1930
the ratio of citizens to students was nine to one, by 1970
it was almost one to one, perhaps contributing to the uneasi-
ness of local citizens.

KSU was relatively quiet during the tumultuous 1960's,
particularly so for a university in the vulnerable "Giant"
category which includes schools whose student body ranges
from 15,000 to 24,000.

But not completely quiet.  On November 13, 1968, members
of the Black United Students and the Students for a Democratic
Society staged a sit-in to protest the presence of recruiters
from the Oakland, California Police Department (long a bitter
foe of the Black Panthers).  The university administration
threatened disciplinary action; in response, some 250 black
students walked off campus, demanding amnesty.  President
White announced that he had been given legal advice to the
effect that the available evidence could not secure convic-
tions; therefore, he said, no charges would be brought.  The
blacks returned.

On April 8, 1969, the Students for a Democratic Society
(SDS) attempted to post a bill of demands in the administration building.  They were met by the campus police.  During
the ensuing scuffle, some of the policemen were struck.
Several students were arrested for assault and battery.  In
addition, the university administration suspended before
hearings the individual students, and revoked without hearings
the SDS charter.  Even though they had little sympathy for the
goals of SDS, nearly half of the students felt that these were

acts of bad faith by the administration because they were perceived as violations of the Student Conduct Code.

On April 16, 1969, a disciplinary hearing for two of the
suspended students was held in the Music and Speech Building.
Supporters of the suspended students demanded that the hearings be made public; they entered the building shouting, "Open
it up or shut it down!" They broke through a metal door on
the third floor where the hearings were being conducted. Law
enforcement personnel sealed all exits, and the Ohio State
Highway Patrol arrested fifty-eight persons. Four SDS leaders
(the original "Kent State Four") were convicted of assault
and battery by a jury trial, and then pleaded guilty to a
charge of inciting to riot. They served six months in the
Portage County jail, being released on April 29, 1970.

A moderate-to-liberal group of faculty and students calling themselves the Concerned Citizens of the KSU Community
(CCC) tried to protest the university's handling of these
events. They were promptly discredited by the administration
and student government leaders.

Meanwhile, many students felt that innocent people had
been entrapped by police during the Music and Speech incident.
Thousands of students conducted a peaceful march across campus
in protest of the suspensions without hearings. A special
report by the university's chapter of the American Association
of University Professors was critical of the administration's
handling of the various events of April.

In the following months of 1969, the firm of R. H. Goettle
and Associates, Inc., of Columbus, Ohio, was retained by the
administration to conduct an opinion survey of the university

community.  During August they conducted interviews with in-
coming freshman (91), undergraduates  (418), graduate students
(76) and faculty members (101).

Some of their findings are pertinent to later events.
The conservative nature of the campus was revealed by the
fact that only four percent of the total sample agreed with
the goals of SDS.  At the same time, only forty-seven percent
"agreed that the administration reacted correctly to campus
disruptions of last April."[7]  Sixteen percent felt that the
administration had been too "soft."  The reasons given by
the rest of those who disapproved were:  "the administration
over-reacted; lack of communication to the student body; and
their policies were inconsistent."[8]

In the "Conclusions and Recommendations" of their report,
the consultants gave the administration high praise.  However,
they noted, "There did appear to be one very significant area
of dissatisfaction on the part of the student body.  Throughout the study appears the word communicate.  More than half
the students feel their views are not listened to or adequately
communicated to the administration.  They do not feel that
adequate channels for communication exist.  This is a problem
that would appear to be soluble, and should be attacked immediately by the administration."[9]

Many specific recommendations for improving communication
were offered; one such recommendation dealt with practices to
be used during a crisis situation because, as they noted,
"Many students said they did not know fact from fiction during
the disturbances."[10]  In a final piece of irony, the consultants found--only nine months prior to the May tragedies--

"Calling the State Highway Patrol or National Guard during disturbances was advocated by 81 percent of the total sample."[11]

To summarize, although the administration received ap-
plause from elements outside the university for its handling
of the April incidents, it had also succeeded in alienating
a large part of the faculty and students--overwhelmingly
unsympathetic to the SDS--for acting in a way perceived to
be inconsistent with the Student Conduct Code, for over-
reacting, for discrediting the CCC and for failing to listen.
Many people were further alienated by the promotion of Dean
Robert Matson, who had played a large role in these matters,
to the newly created position of Vice President for Student
Affairs.

The administration did respond to the Goettler study,
however, by creating the position of Coordinator of Internal
Communication.  Gerald Hayes, a KSU graduate, was appointed
to the position during the fall of 1969.  By May he had succeeded in identifying and coordinating the media available
for one-way, downward-directed communication such as *For Your
Information* (FYI), a weekly bulletin directed from the administration to the faculty.  Little was accomplished, however, to
facilitate upward-directed communication.  Indeed, by its
actions of April--particularly by driving the SDS underground-
the administration had made its own job more difficult.  As
two Vice Presidents later told us, upward communication from
and about radical students ("intelligence," if you will) became "harder to come by."

Nonetheless, the academic year of '69-'70 was so quiet
at Kent State that one Vice President told us, "Until Cambodia

I thought we would make the year.  Then it became a question
of, 'When will it happen?'"

In late April a group of students staged a guerilla
theater production on the Commons.  They had publicly announced
their plans to protest American actions in Vietnam by napalm-
ing a dog.  A large crowd showed up on the announced date
(including university police, county police and even the
County Prosecutor, Ronald Kane).  The drama was so ironically
effective that the crowd "prevented" the students from napalm-
ing the dog--even drawing enthusiastic praise from the Prosecutor for their responsible behavior.

It really began to "happen" on May 1, 1970.  On Thursday,
April 30, the senior author had lunch with a prominent Kent
businessman.  The businessman expressed his distaste for the
war and his deep concern with the Cambodian invasion.  Further,
he anticipated serious difficulties on college campuses if
President Nixon's speech scheduled for television that night
did not adequately justify this apparent reversal of his policy
of "winding down the war."  This man's business establishment
was one of fifteen to be "hit" on the following night.

*Friday, May 1*

A peaceful, half-serious and half-jocular rally was
attended by an estimated 500 persons on the Commons at noon.
The acronym of the group sponsoring the event (World Historians
Opposed to Racism and Exploitation) suggests the mixed feel-
ings of some of the participants.  A copy of the Constitution
was buried, signifying that it had been "murdered" when the
President sent troops to Cambodia without the approval of
Congress.

Several interviewees reported that they heard at this
rally mention of "action" and "street dances" which might
"happen" in the city that night.  Students involved in practic
teaching at schools off the campus were also informed.  Indeed
members of the Student Affairs division circulated among downtown bars that evening because of warnings about a "street
scene," but they left a few minutes before the trouble began.

The administration, however, was probably more concerned
about a rally planned by blacks for mid-afternoon Friday.
Perhaps 400 blacks attended the rally.  After the meeting
ended without disturbance (and after listening to all of the
available "intelligence"), the President of the university
felt sufficiently confident about the situation to depart for
Iowa to visit his sister-in-law and attend a Sunday meeting
of the American College Testing Program, of which he was an
officer.

On a typical Friday afternoon and evening there is a
steady stream of traffic leaving and entering the city of
Kent.  Kent State has long been called a "suitcase university,"
so called because many students leave the campus on Friday
for a weekend at home.  At the same time, Kent's large number
of bars catering to young people attracts swarms of young
people from all over the region.  On a typical Friday night,
one can drive through the downtown area and observe lengthy
queues of young people waiting to be admitted to the packed
bars.  Loud rock music, some from live bands, emanates from
the bars.

Friday night, May 1, was unseasonably warm, but quiet
until about 11:00 p.m., when a motorcycle gang, "The Chosen

Few," began to perform tricks on their bikes for the people lining North Water Street--where a half dozen of the bars are located.   Soon the young people began to jeer at and pelt passing police cruisers.   The undermanned Kent police requested help from other agencies.

A bonfire was built in the street.   Rocks and other objects were hurled through store windows.   A few items were stolen.   At 12:30 a.m., Mayor LeRoy Satrom declared a State of Civil Emergency and ordered the bars closed.

A combined force of fifteen city police and fifteen sheriff's deputies moved the mob (estimates range between 300 and 500) down Water Street to Main Street--the main intersection of the city.   Unfortunately, the Mayor's order enlarged the mob with angry drinkers emptied from downtown bars, many of whom were ignorant of the "trashing."

A number of persons slipped away via side streets as the mob was driven up Main Street toward the campus.   At this point occurred the first major communication breakdown.   The Kent Police Department had a total force of twenty-two men while the KSU Police Department had a total force of thirty-three men, making the latter the *largest and best equipped full-time* security force in Portage County.

The city police and administration felt that they had a firm agreement with campus security forces to cover such a contingency as they faced at that moment; i.e., they fully expected, once having driven the mob to the edge of the campus, the university police would come to their assistance if not assume full control of the situation.   Why this agreement was violated is not quite clear.   The Scranton Commission explained it by concluding that city police "did not know that students were simultaneously congregating on campus and that the University Police Chief Donald L. Schwartzmiller had decided to use his men to guard campus buildings. A small amount of property damage was done on campus, including a broken window at the ROTC building."[12] The city police, however, faced the same dilemma: having committed their entire on-duty force to the mob, they were unable to respond to requests for help from local citizens (e.g., a machine shop was broken into); the rest of the city was unprotected.

The campus Director of Safety, Chester Williams, had been promoted to that position in 1968, after serving eleven years as Business Manager for Athletics. Williams, who has since been relieved of his security responsibilities, was out of town that night. His campus security officer, Donald Schwartzmiller, was notified at home of the difficulties some time after midnight. Sources within the KSU police department revealed to us that it had been decided to send four men to help the city police, but the order was countermanded by Schwartzmiller when he arrived on campus. City sources indicate that they first saw and talked to Schwartzmiller some time between 2:30 and 3:00 a.m. City and university sources indicated that several campus policemen later apologized because their force had failed to help on Friday night.

City officials were infuriated by the broken agreement. They wondered about the same question posed to us by a top university official: "Why were the nineteen university police men in full riot gear at the stadium never called in to action The already tenuous relationship between city and university deteriorated rapidly.

The mob finally drifted away, although city officials reported having "a problem as late as 3:30 [a.m.]." Fifteen arrests were made that night and early morning--mainly on charges of disorderly conduct and resisting arrest. The Chamber of Commerce later revealed that $10,000 damage had been done during the rampage.

One of the original Kent State Four was seen in downtown Kent that night (off-duty policemen work as bartenders), but according to the Scranton Commission, "The FBI uncovered no evidence that the Kent State 4 were involved in planning or directing any of the events of the May 1-4 weekend."[13] The city was convinced, however, that the problems were planned by "outside agitators" who wore red headbands.

How our student subjects first learned about the events of Friday night is indicated in Table 1. We have divided the sample of students into categories of on-campus (those who were residing in dorms, or residence halls, as they are now called), off-campus (those who were living in apartments, rooms, or with their family in Kent) and commuters. The dependency of the commuters on the mass media is illustrated clearly. Also, students living in Kent were able to learn faster by means of face-to-face communication with their fellow students. The importance of the oral communication of such information is further emphasized when one adds the unknown word-of-mouth sources to the student sources. The result accounts for the source of over fifty-five percent of the student subjects.

### HOW FIRST LEARNED OF FRIDAY EVENTS

Students  N=225

|            | Eye-Witness | Stu-dents | Radio | News-paper | TV | WOM* | Totals |
|------------|-------------|-----------|-------|------------|-----|------|--------|
| On-Campus  | 4           | 58        | 13    | 7          | 9   | 10   | 101    |
| Off-Campus | 9           | 21        | 12    | 5          | 3   | 22   | 72     |
| Commuters  | 0           | 5         | 18    | 10         | 10  | 9    | 52     |
| Totals     | 13          | 84        | 43    | 22         | 22  | 41   | 225    |

*Word-of-mouth from unknown sources

TABLE 1

It is interesting to compare the findings of the faculty (N=120) and department chairmen (N=29) to the students (Table 2). Like the category of commuting students, the faculty and chairmen were far more dependent upon the mass media than were the students residing in Kent. The faculty was isolated from the students' face-to-face network: nor did they play a significant role in keeping their colleagues, i.e., each other, informed. In addition, there were widespread complaints in our interviews because the chairmen and faculty were not informed through the official university channels.

### HOW FIRST LEARNED OF FRIDAY EVENTS

|                       | Eye-Witness | Stu-dents | Radio | News-paper | TV | Faculty | WOM | Totals |
|-----------------------|-------------|-----------|-------|------------|-----|---------|-----|--------|
| Students              | 13          | 84        | 43    | 22         | 22  | 0       | 41  | 225    |
| Faculty and Chairmen  | 3           | 4         | 46    | 20         | 7   | 14      | 55  | 149    |
| Totals                | 16          | 88        | 89    | 42         | 29  | 14      | 96  | 374    |

TABLE 2

Because the events of Friday night continued into Saturday morning, it was difficult to tabulate just when our subjects first heard about them.  It is obvious that the commuting students and faculty were much slower to learn the facts than were the students residing in Kent--no doubt because of their isolation from the students' oral network.

Various staff members, on the other hand, were informed quite early.  For example, of the twenty-five members of the Student Affairs division we interviewed (people concerned with dormitories, student conduct, student government and the whole range of student services), all but one were informed by Saturday--most of them by early Saturday.  Of the twelve members of the Business and Finance division we interviewed (people concerned with maintenance, the "business" aspects of the university and--most importantly to this part of the study-- university security), four were made aware immediately Friday night and all the rest knew by Saturday.  Of the six people interviewed in the division of Administration (people concerned with internal communication, public relations and community relations), all but one were immediately informed. Despite the fact that most staff members were early-informed, the academic sector had to fend for itself in keeping up with the fast-moving events.

### Saturday, May 2

The tension continued.  City and administration officials had slept little the night before.  Rumors competed for credulity.  Merchants reported that they had been threatened with damage unless they displayed anti-war signs in their windows. (And some were reportedly threatened by "concerned citizens"

if they did display them.)  Destruction of campus buildings,
notably the Army ROTC building, was also rumored.

Mayor LeRoy Satrom was in an extremely difficult position.
He had been in office only four months.  Responsible for the
safety of Kent's 30,000 citizens and their property, he had
few options open to him.  His city police force, even augmented
by additional men from other Portage County law enforcement
agencies, was inadequate to cope with the kind of violence
rumored.  He could not turn to the State Highway Patrol (preferred by the university to handle such situations) because
their jurisdiction extends only to state highways and state
property.  Given the lack of cooperation from university police, he could turn only to the Ohio National Guard for help
in protecting the city.

The Mayor had apprised Governor James A. Rhodes' office
of the situation at 12:47 a.m., just a few minutes after
having declared a State of Civil Emergency.  The Governor's
office alerted the Ohio Adjutant General, Major General
Sylvester T. Del Corso.  Del Corso, in turn, dispatched a
National Guard liaison officer, Lt. Charles J. Barnette, to
Kent.

Lt. Barnette found it necessary to serve also as a liaison
between the city and university.  There was practically no
direct communication between the two administrations at that
time.

Contributing to this lack of communication was an authority
crisis on campus.  "We were a driverless car racing downhill
without brakes," one department chairman told us later in an
interview.

On page ninety-eight of the *Academic Policy Book* the then operative "Emergency Operations" were specified: "In the absence of the President, emergency decisions which cannot await his return shall be the responsibility of the Vice President and Provost; in the event of his absence also, the Vice President for Business and Finance; in the event of his absence also, the Executive Dean for Educational and Student Services [former title of the Vice President for Student Affairs]; in the event of his absence also, the Vice President for University Relations and Development [former title of Vice President for Administration]."

These clear-cut contingencies were obfuscated, however, by several factors. First, the man named to assume authority during the President's absence, Vice President and Provost Louis Harris, was ill and *unaware that the President had left town.* In addition, there were four categories of emergencies which specified additional chains-of-authority.

The Vice President for Business and Finance was to assume authority in times of "physical plant or mechanical breakdown with reference to fire, electrical, plumbing or heating failures or the like." The Vice President and Provost was to assume authority in case of "matters of weather or similar developments leading to the possibility of suspension of classes. . ." The Vice President for Student Affairs was to assume authority during times of "student demonstrations or irregular behavior." The Vice President for Administration, during a "national or state disaster of which war, bombing, presidential assassination, national hysteria" was the cause, was authorized to "confer with appropriate national, state or

local officials in order to advise the President of the participation of the University."

Obviously, these "emergency" contingencies are incompat
with the "absence" contingencies.  If the "emergency" contin
gencies take precedence over the "absence" contingencies, as
appears to be the case, the university could be subject to tl
indignity of a scramble for power dependent on the categori-
zation of the kind of emergency facing the university.  (In
reality, one Vice President told us that the emergency contingencies were created because of the President's "inabilit]
to make a decision during a crisis.")

Unhappily enough, these contingencies were interpreted
in different ways by the principals.  One Vice President, fo]
example, said in interview that regardless of the formal sta1
ment, the informal agreement was that all decisions--even
during emergencies--were made by "cabinet consensus" (the
President's cabinet included the four Vice Presidents, an
Assistant for Planning and the Executive Assistant to the
President, Ronald Beer).  Two other Vice Presidents each fel1
that the responsibility was squarely and solely his own.  Th¢
fourth felt that he shared the authority with another, that
"no one was acting as President in his absence."

Many of our interviewees reflected the confusion and
anxiety which existed within the university; the "driverless
car" was difficult also for outsiders to cope with.  The
President was out of town, as was the Vice President for Administration, Ronald Roskens, whose division was responsible
for internal communication, public relations and community
relations as well as for conferring with "appropriate nation;

state or local officials."

Disappointed with the university's lack of cooperation during the previous night's disturbances, the Mayor had no personal relationships with remaining administrators by which to alleviate the situation. There is evidence that he, like many others, did not know who was in charge "on the hill." Therefore, during this critical period (and for some time after) the city and the university simply were not speaking with and listening to each other directly. This was extremely unfortunate.

Two Vice Presidents were on the campus Saturday when Lt. Charles J. Barnette, liaison officer of the Ohio National Guard arrived. They were Vice President for Student Affairs, Robert Matson, who was to assume authority during "student demonstrations and irregular behavior"; and Vice President for Business and Finance, Richard Dunn, who was to assume authority during a "fire" or other physical plant breakdown--and under whose supervision the university security forces rested. Emergency operations had not been planned; frankly, they were "played by ear."

Lt. Barnette told university officials that if the Ohio National Guard were called into action, it would be in three "phases": (1) the troops already on duty for the truck strike would go on alert in Akron's Rubber Bowl (a football stadium); (2) the troops would be transported to bivouac in Kent at either Wall Elementary School or Fred Fuller Park; (3) the troops would go into action, making no distinction between city and campus. University officials came away from the meeting thinking that they would be kept fully informed at each step of the procedure.

The Mayor had that morning formally proclaimed his State of Civil Emergency coupled with a curfew from 8:00 p.m. to 6:00 a.m., which prohibited pedestrian traffic and, as broad cast over radio, warned people not to "loiter in your car." The new administration did not yet realize the limits of its power and agreed to a 1:00 a.m., curfew on the campus.

At about the same time that the Mayor was issuing his proclamation, university officials were acquiring a "John Doe" injunction which in effect made anyone participating in violence on campus in contempt of court.

The injunction, which was posted on buildings and doors throughout the campus, *did not include a ban on assembly.* In addition, 12,000 copies of a "Student Information Sheet" signed by Matson and the Student Body President, Frank Frisina were distributed on campus. The sheet explained the injunction but noted that it "does not prevent peaceful assembly- demonstration, dissent or movement about the campus." The sheet also explained the Mayor's curfew, but did *not* note the 1:00 a.m., campus curfew, simply warning that "the curfew does not apply to the Kent campus proper, but as soon as you step off-campus after 8:00 p.m. you are in violation of the curfew." The warning was prophetic.

Exactly at 1:30 p.m., the campus FM radio station, WKSU, carried the first of several announcements about the curfew. It manifests a communication breakdown either within the city administration or between City Police and the radio station. Listing the "specific rules as ascertained by WKSU Radio after consultation with the Kent City Police and the Kent State

University Police," the copy concluded with the misinformation that "the above rules do *not* apply for students remaining on the Kent State campus, and students will have the same freedom as always.  But only while remaining on campus.  Students may not walk on city streets."  Again, the 1:00 a.m. campus curfew was not noted.

It is not surprising that our interviewees reported widespread confusion about curfews, and that sixty to seventy arrests were made Saturday night; most of these were for curfew violations, and many of those arrested were people who had attended campus activities such as the film festival in the university auditorium.  The entire cast of a play was arrested, but released without charge after a professor known to the Mayor intervened.  As one freshman told us, "I wasn't sure of the time of the curfew because it kept changing."  A co-ed said that she called the KSU P.D. Saturday afternoon, but even they were "hazy."

In a meeting at 1:00 p.m., attended by Vice President Matson, Faculty Ombudsman Harold Kitner, a popular University Professor Glenn Frank and others, the concept of using faculty members as Peace Marshals was considered.  Deciding to permit the marshals to rely only on persuasion, the group designated Professor Frank to round up faculty members and blue armbands by which to designate them as marshals.

Lt. Barnette had given Mayor Satrom a 5:00 p.m. deadline on his decision whether or not to call out the Guard--already on duty to protect against violence in the wildcat Teamster strike.  With the Highway Patrol unavailable, with the sheriff's deputies unavailable, with the KSU security forces unavailable,

Satrom had no alternative but to call the Guard.

At 5:28 p.m., the Mayor called the Governor's office in Columbus. He spoke with John McElroy, administrative assistant to Governor Rhodes. McElroy called General Del Corso and instructed him to return the call to Mayor Satrom. McElr called the Governor to secure authorization for the commitmen of the Guard. This was accomplished. *The university was not informed* of these decisions, which was to divide further the two administrations.

General Del Corso returned the call to Mayor Satrom at 5:35 p.m., informing him that troops would be available. The General then ordered the Guardsmen in the Akron area to be pu on alert. About forty minutes later, Del Corso informed the duty officer at National Guard headquarters, Colonel John Simmons, that he and the Assistant Adjutant General, Robert Canterbury, were leaving for Kent; that if Simmons were to receive another request from Mayor Satrom while he and Canter bury were on the way he was to dispatch troops from the Rubbe Bowl in Akron to bivouac at Wall School in Kent.

An aide to Vice President Matson was sent to inquire of campus security officials whether or not they had sufficient manpower to keep order on the campus.

"No sweat," was the reply.

The central portion of the KSU campus is a large grassy field called the Commons. By tradition, rallies and assembli are signalled by the ringing of the Victory Bell, which once served a locomotive, but had since been remounted on a brick structure at the south edge of the Commons, just opposite the wooden, barrack-type, Army ROTC building, where the next serious confrontation was to take place, and at the bottom of a grassy slope at whose acclivity stood Taylor Hall--where the final, fatal confrontation would take place.

A crowd had gathered at the Bell by 7:30 p.m.  The university Police Chief, Donald Schwartzmiller, requested assistance from the Highway Patrol, with whom he had formerly served.  The patrol explained its policy; i.e., that it would respond only when notified of concrete bases for arrests. The practice of the patrol, once notified, was to dispatch the necessary patrolmen to the Highway Patrol Post in nearby Ravenna, Ohio.  Once assembled, they were then bussed to the campus in Kent.  This operation required *at least* one and one-half hours from the moment of notification to the moment of the arrival of the patrolmen.  This should make obvious the clear principle that under such policies, the Highway Patrol could only be useful as a supplemental arresting force; that other forces would be required to contain the people responsible for disturbances for *at least ninety minutes after an "arrestable" offense*.  Thus, the university's dependence on the patrol was unrealistic.

The crowd abruptly left the Commons and began a tortuous route through several dormitories, trying to recruit supporters. They were closely observed by the faculty marshals and campus police.  Shortly after 8:00 p.m., they marched down the hills around the Commons directly toward the two-story, wooden ROTC building.  Railroad flares were hurled at the building, as well as rocks and other missiles.  One person set fire to a curtain which blazed briefly--and then went out.  "It was an inept attempt at arson," observed one eyewitness.  The

building did not begin to burn until 8:45 p.m., and as the
Scranton Commission Report noted, only "a dozen or so persons
appeared to have made active efforts to set the building
afire. . ."[14]  Why did the campus police, whose headquarters
were 200 yards from the ROTC building, fail to intercede?
One top university official gave this explanation:  "We had
men at the President's house and the Liquid Crystals Institut
[a research facility with defense contracts, long a target of
the SDS].  We try not to go into a crowd when we think it
might be inflammatory [*sic!*]."

At about 9:00 p.m., a truck from the City Fire Departmen
arrived in response to a call from the university police.  Fo
the second time in as many nights, the *KSU P.D. violated a
long-standing agreement with the city;* i.e., they failed to
provide police protection for city firemen entering the campu
to fight a fire.  Then firemen were pelted with rocks.  Their
hoses were cut by knives, ice picks and a machete, clearly
indicative that some of the protestors came with more than a
peaceful rally in mind.  They, the firemen, were forced to
flee.  Again city officials were infuriated with the university.

Only after the firemen had left did the university polic
appear.  They marched up in riot gear and fired tear gas into
the mob.  The mob dispersed.

At 8:35 p.m., Mayor Satrom renewed his request for help
to Columbus.  Acting under the orders given by General Del
Corso, Colonel Simmons called Akron and ordered the troops to
Kent.  Phase two of the plan outlined to the university by Lt
Barnette was effected.  Again the university was not informed

Generals Del Corso and Canterbury arrived in Kent at 9:30 p.m., when the sky was bright from the ROTC blaze. After a briefing by Mayor Satrom, they ordered one group of troopers to prevent students from entering the downtown area, while another group was sent with city firemen in their second attempt to put out the fire. Phase three had been effected. Again, the university was not informed.

Before they realized the Guard was on campus, university officials including security personnel discussed the possibility of calling the Guard. As one top official told us, "We probably would have called them anyway." Indeed, Williams and Schwartzmiller admitted having called the Guard. Who called the Guard on to the campus in this case, then, is an academic question. Also, it should be remembered that the National Guard first moved on to the campus to perform a function which would have been unnecessary if the university police had met the conditions of their long-standing agreement with the city; i.e., if they had provided protection for the firemen when they first came to extinguish the ROTC fire.

Part of the crowd dispersed by the campus police had moved in the direction of downtown Kent. When advised of this, Vice President Matson "told the Guard that the matter was no longer in his hands because the crowd was now off campus and in the town."[15] Guardsmen prevented the students from entering the downtown area. We say "students," but it is wise to consider this statement in the Scranton Commission Report: "Information developed by an FBI investigation of the ROTC building fire indicates that, of those who participated actively, a significant proportion were not Kent State students."[16]

The Guard's entry to the campus was followed by sheriff'
deputies and highway patrolmen.  The ROTC building could not
be saved; the university estimated its loss, including con-
tents, at $86,000.

The Guard established its headquarters in the Board of
Trustee's Conference Room in the administration building.
Students continued to roam the campus lighting small fires.
The Guard moved out, clearing the campus with the liberal use
of tear gas.  Many students, faculty and even faculty marshal
told us that they had come into contact with the gas.  Some
students spent the night in whatever dormitory had been neare
when they encountered the Guard and the gas.  The security of
the campus was now in the hands of the Ohio National Guard.

When and how our subjects first learned of the events of
Saturday, May 2, is shown in Table 3.  Not surprisingly, the

WHEN FIRST LEARNED OF SATURDAY EVENTS

|  | Sat. | Sun. | Mon. | Total |
|---|---|---|---|---|
| On-Campus | 73 | 27 | 1 | 101 |
| Off-Campus | 44 | 27 | 1 | 72 |
| Commuters | 22 | 23 | 7 | 52 |
| Faculty and Chairmen | 88 | 54 | 7 | 149 |
| Staff | 32 | 8 | 3 | 43 |
| Totals | 259 | 139 | 19 | 417 |

TABLE 3

on-campus students and staff members (from the three non-
academic divisions) were the earliest to learn:  the former
because the actions of Saturday were close to their residence

halls, the latter because of their involvement in police work, student activities and in operating the university's command post.  The commuting students, faculty and chairmen were the last to know.  A disturbingly high percentage of commuters (fourteen percent) did not know about the fire until Monday.

Table 4 presents just *how* our subjects first heard about Saturday's events.  Again the faculty and commuting students-- lacking the cohesive, face-to-face network of resident students

HOW FIRST LEARNED OF SATURDAY EVENTS

| | Eye-Witness | Stu-dents | Radio | News-papers | TV | Faculty | WOM | Total |
|---|---|---|---|---|---|---|---|---|
| On-Campus | 30 | 26 | 15 | 8 | 9 | 0 | 13 | 101 |
| Off-Campus | 6 | 15 | 16 | 5 | 6 | 0 | 24 | 72 |
| Commuters | 2 | 2 | 9 | 17 | 20 | 0 | 2 | 52 |
| Faculty and Chairmen | 21 | 3 | 42 | 16 | 11 | 17 | 39 | 149 |
| Staff | 19 | 0 | 4 | 1 | 2 | 0 | 17 | 43 |
| Total | 78 | 46 | 86 | 47 | 48 | 17 | 95 | 417 |

TABLE 4

and staff--were more dependent than those groups on the mass media.  Radio emerged as the most significant of the mass media for all but one group (commuters,) and particularly so for the faculty and chairmen.  By this time, many faculty members had become alerted to the difficulties and were keeping close to the radio.  (Nonetheless, the mass media first informed only forty-three percent of our subjects which seems unusually low for a weekend.)

Saturday night's events were viewed by a high percentage (almost nineteen percent) of eye witnesses.  This is a slight

overestimate because we classified those who reported seeing
the flames of the ROTC building at a distance in that category.  Nonetheless, it does give one a new perspective on mob
size estimates when realizing that forty-four percent of our
sample of staff members were present and, hopefully, not participating in arson.

For the first time faculty members begin to emerge as a
source--but only for each other!  No one other than a faculty
member reported first hearing about Saturday's events from a
faculty member, although some of the tabulations in the word-
of-mouth category could easily have been professors.  (In fact
some of the WOM sources for the staff group were staff colleagues.)  Again, there is no evidence that formal channels
were activated to reach the academic sector.

### Sunday, May 3

"Perhaps the principal contribution of the troubled
years," wrote Historian Shriver about KSU's problems of the
late twenties, "was the lesson that education and politics
cannot be mixed without serious injury to education."[17]  The
mixture in May of 1970 made for an injury that was almost
fatal.

The Governor of Ohio, James Rhodes, arrived in Kent on
Sunday morning.  Unable to succeed himself after eight years
as Governor, Rhodes was locked in a close primary election
with Congressman Robert Taft for the Republican nomination to
the United State Senate.  Running behind Taft (perhaps because
of the *Life* magazine article accusing him of misconduct) polls
reported in Northern Ohio newspapers showed his stiff stands
against campus unrest to result in gains in populous Cuyahoga

County.

The gray-haired Governor promptly called a news conference. The rhetoric he directed undoubtedly toward Ohio voters would further alienate members of the Kent State University community. The Kent disturbances, he said, were probably "the most vicious form of campus-oriented violence yet perpetrated" in Ohio, and he pledged to his listeners that "we are going to employ every force of law that we have under our authority.  We are going to employ every weapon possible."

"These people," Rhodes continued, "just move from one campus to the other and terrorize a community.  They're worse than the brown shirts and the Communist element and also the night riders and the vigilantes.  They're the worst type of people that we harbor in America."

His penultimate remark was:  "We are going to eradicate the problem--we're not going to treat the symptoms."

Ohio Highway Patrol Superintendent Chiaramonte spoke next. Anticipating that the next phase of the disturbances would be for the demonstrators to start sniping, he said:  "They can expect us to return fire."  Mayor Satrom also spoke, warning that "We will take all necessary and I repeat, all necessary action to maintain order."

After the news conference, the youthful County Prosecutor, Ronald J. Kane, suggested to Governor Rhodes that the university be closed.  Rhodes disagreed, arguing that this would be playing into the hands of the SDS.

A university airplane had been sent to Iowa to pick up President White.  Governor Rhodes delayed his own takeoff in order to advise President White.  "Keep it open," was his message.

During the press conference, Rhodes had said, "We are
going to ask for an injunction. . .equivalent to a state of
emergency." According to the Scranton Commission, "There is
no official record that such an injunction was ever sought or
obtained."[18]

Vice President for Student Affairs Robert Matson had attended the press conference and set his executive assistant,
John Huffman, to work on the definition of such a "state of em
gency." Huffman, an attorney, talked to a Guard officer and
"received the impression that the state of emergency permitted
'no gatherings or rallies at all.'"[19] *This was a fatal misint
pretation.* The only proclamation in effect was Mayor Satrom's
State of Civil Emergency--which did not prohibit assembly.

Based solely on Huffman's misinterpretation, Matson and
Frank Frisina (student body President) released 12,000 copies
of "A special message to the University community." The leaflet began with the statement that the destruction of the two
previous days had led to the "Governor's imposition of a state
of emergency encompassing both the city of Kent and the University."

It continued:

> The Governor, through the National Guard, has assume
> legal control of the campus and the city of Kent. As
> currently defined the state of emergency has established
> the following:
>
> 1. Prohibited all forms of outdoor demonstrations and
>    rallys (*sic*.) - peaceful or otherwise;
>
> 2. Empowered the National Guard to make arrests;
>
> 3. A curfew is in effect for the city from 8 p.m. to
>    6 a.m. and an on-campus curfew of 1:00 a.m. has
>    been ordered by the National Guard.
>
> The above will remain in effect until altered or

removed by order of the Governor.

The message went on to say, "We are most thankful that thus far there has been no loss of life."

This document forced the final, fatal confrontation between the students and the Guard. According to the Scranton Commission, General Canterbury later cited this leaflet "as one source of his authority for banning rallies."[20]

President White broadcast his own statement, the point of which was: "Events have taken decisions out of our hands." Several similar statements had been made by university administrators, some of which were even included in the Matson-Frisina leaflet. This was an inaccurate and misleading position. The Guard was already beginning to think of withdrawing. The Guard apparently had no interest in "running" the university--its sole interest being in peacekeeping. Even there the Guard would later permit university administration to participate in such decisions as whether or not assemblies should be prohibited. It was as if the university was attempting to force responsibility on to the Governor and the Guard. "The university lay down and bared its throat to the enemy by this posture," one highly qualified university observer told us.

During late afternoon, a group of twenty-three faculty issued a statement deploring the Guard's presence and the Governor's inflammatory remarks. They deplored also the destructive behavior of students, but asked that such acts be viewed in the context of the Indo-Chinese War. A group of sixty faculty members requested President White to call a full faculty meeting. White declined on the ground that only the Faculty Senate could call such a meeting.

Generals Del Corso and Canterbury had left town on Sunda
morning, leaving Colonel Harold Finley in charge of the Guard
The afternoon was quiet, although many students returning from
a weekend away were shocked to find the campus completely
circled by Guardsmen and their military vehicles. Some, however, adopted a festive mood, placing flowers in the Guardsmen's rifle barrels and kidding them good-naturedly about
their unusual duty. Students began gathering at 8:00 p.m.
Shortly before 9:00, the campus police and Highway Patrol
became concerned about the size of the growing crowd; they
recommended to Colonel Finley that he rescind the 1:00 a.m.
curfew, and impose a 9:00 p.m. curfew. Colonel Finley so
decided, and Major Jones literally read the Riot Act to the
crowd, giving the crowd five minutes to disperse.

The crowd failed to respond to the order and were prompt]
gassed. Part of them headed for the President's house, others
for Prentice Gate (a campus landmark since 1935, it is the
entrance to the campus at Main and Lincoln and had been the
scene of the confrontation on Friday night). A large crowd
sat down in the intersection where they requested to speak to
Mayor Satrom and President White.

An unidentified young man using a police bullhorn incorrectly informed the crowd that Mayor Satrom was on his way
to discuss their demands, and that an effort was being made
to ask White to do the same.

The crowd was later informed that White and Satrom would
not meet with them, even though the latter was on the way to
the scene. According to the Scranton Commission, the students
previously non-violent, "became hostile. They felt that they

had been double-crossed.   They cursed the guardsmen and police and threw rocks at them.   Tear gas was fired and the crowd ran back from the gate across the campus lawn."[21]   Some of our sources said that the tear gas was fired without warning. Regardless, in the melee which ensued three Guardsmen were injured by various missiles while several students sustained minor cuts from bayonets.

By the time General Canterbury returned to Kent--shortly before midnight--the Guard had swept the campus with bayonets, gas and the searchlight probes of helicopters.   More than fifty persons were arrested Sunday, bringing the three day total to more than 100; local and county jails were straining to contain the young people.

A curious phenomenon was revealed by the questions we asked concerning how and when our subjects first learned of Sunday night's events.   Forty four of the sample of faculty and chairmen (almost thirty percent) *could not recall what happened*.   Thirty of the sample of students (over thirteen percent) *could not recall what happened*.   In fact, subjects often asked the interviewer what had happened on Sunday.   This category did not appear in the subject's answers about the events before and after Sunday.   In addition, many of those who did recall something of those events were unsure when and how they learned of them (therefore, we are skeptical of the data and have not presented them here).   Indeed, many incorrectly inferred that the situation had cooled down because they had not heard anything about what had happened Sunday.

Several hypotheses can be advanced to explain these facts.   First, some employees of the mass media may take a

day of rest, making the media less effective in reporting news
made on Sunday night than on the other nights of the week.
Second, some students and faculty may have turned their attention toward preparations for Monday's classes.  Third, the
magnitude of the killings on Monday may have been so overwhelming that they blotted out any memory of Sunday's events,
particularly for those who were not eye witnesses.  Perhaps
it was a combination of factors.

*Monday, May 4*

It was about 8:30 a.m., when one of the authors crossed
the Guard's line around the perimeter of the campus.  As he
entered the Music and Speech Building he noticed broken glass
from a shattered door.  Posted on another door was a copy of
the "John Doe" injunction which prohibited destruction on the
campus (but which did *not* prohibit assembly).  There was a
hand scrawled announcement on a first floor bulletin board
calling for a rally on the Commons at noon.  He wondered
whether the undated sign had been posted for the Friday rally
or for one on Monday.

Because of the extraordinary situation, he asked a
secretary to call the Provost's office to determine whether or
not classes had been cancelled.  She learned that classes
were meeting as usual.  It did not occur to him--and to many
others--to ask whether or not his right to assemble had been
prohibited.  As many of our interviewees asked, rhetorically,
"Is not a class an assembly of sorts?"  This is an appropriate
question when one considers that there were classes with many
hundreds of students meeting on Monday.

President White had already met with his cabinet (7:00 a.m.) and the executive committee of the Faculty Senate (8:00 a.m.).   In the latter conference he agreed to meet with the full faculty in a late afternoon meeting.  Gerald Hayes, Coordinator of Internal Communication, was preparing a bulletin for the faculty (*FYI*) explaining the weekend's events. The closing of the campus later in the day would cancel the faculty meeting, and prevent Mr. Hayes from distributing his bulletin.

The Education Building was evacuated early in the morning by order of the KSU P.D. because of a telephoned bomb threat.  The campus police failed to call back with an "all-clear," leaving faculty, students and staff with an individual decision to make about re-entering.  The Business Administration building was thrown into considerable confusion by a bomb threat.  The University High School and other buildings were also threatened with bombings.  The formal channels of the university still had not begun to function.

A crucial meeting had been called by General Canterbury for 10:00 a.m.  Attending the meeting were the General and the legal officer of the ONG, Major William R. Shrimp, President White, Vice President Matson, Major Donald E. Manly of the Ohio State Highway Patrol, Mayor Satrom and the city's Safety Director, Paul Hershey.

Several items were on the agendum.  It was clear by this time that there was widespread confusion about the inconsistent campus curfews.  It was decided to amend the Mayor's Proclamation of Civil Emergency by having the 8:00 p.m. to 6:00 a.m. curfew apply equally to the campus and the community.

University representatives were relieved to hear General
Canterbury express his desire to withdraw the Guard, but the
Mayor--who had officially requested their presence--insisted
that a dangerous situation persisted.

The discussion then turned to how the noon rally should
be handled.  General Canterbury asked the university representatives whether or not it should be permitted.  The public
testimony and published accounts of this discussion are
contradictory.

Our sources, however, seem to have cleared the confusion
The university advised against permitting the rally because
to do so would be *inconsistent with the leaflet* which had
been distributed the day before.  It was argued that consis-
tency from day to day on such matters was a "must."  It was
also argued that if such a reversal of the prohibitions were
made, it would have to be announced "ahead of time by at
least two hours."  It was at least 11:00 a.m. when the matter
was being discussed.  Students were already assembling on the
Commons.  The meeting was closed on the understanding that the
assembly would not be permitted.  General Canterbury left the
meeting for Guard headquarters which had been moved from the
Board of Trustees Conference room to a gymnasium attached to
the Administration Building.  President White, his assistant
and some of his Vice Presidents met for lunch at the Brown
Derby, a restaurant on the outskirts of the city of Kent.

The crucial importance of the Matson-Frisina "special
message to the University community" should now become clear.
Based solely upon a conversation between John Huffman, attorne
and assistant to Matson, and Major Jones of the ONG, it

inaccurately stated that the "Governor's imposition of a state of emergency" had "prohibited all forms of outdoor rallys (*sic.*)," and "that the Governor, through the National Guard, has assumed legal control of the campus and the city of Kent." If the document had been true, it apparently would have been news to General Canterbury and the legal officer of the ONG, Major Shrimp, because *they allowed university officials to participate in the decision as to whether or not the rally scheduled for noon should be prohibited.* It is inconceivable that the question could have otherwise been raised in the 10:00 a.m. meeting. It is also significant that it was Mayor Satrom's proclamation which was amended in regard to the campus curfew, not the "Governor, through the National Guard," who had "legal control of the campus."

In short, this inaccurate document--which was produced by an "impression" formed by a university attorney during a conversation with a Guardsman *other than the ONG legal officer*-- was later used by the university *and* the ONG to justify the prohibition of assembly. To complete the irony, the document was almost completely ineffective (as we shall see) in achieving its stated purpose as a vehicle of communication, as "A special message to the University community."

By 11:45 a.m., more than 500 people had assembled on the Commons. It is not our purpose to reconstruct the killings themselves. We can add little to what is already published. Let our account suffice to say that even if the Guard or the city or the university had the right to prohibit what was at this point a peaceful assembly--a legal question yet to be settled--the tactics used were absurd. Once the Guard, with

loaded weapons, ordered the peaceful crowd to disperse, it
became outraged, obscene and violent:  outraged that its
"turf" had been "invaded," outraged that a basic constitution
right had been denied; obscene in chanting its now hackneyed
slogan of "One, two, three, four, we don't want your fucking
war"; violent in casting back at Guardsmen the tear gas
canisters lobbed at them--along with sticks and stones and,
of course, the dirty words.

But what is to be gained by charging such a crowd with
bayonets and gas in the wide, windy spaces of a large univers.
campus?  Once dispersed they can whirl around and behind a
small group of men constrained by tight military formations,
gathering again when the gas meant to disperse them is itself
dispersed by the fourteen mile-per-hour winds.  Perhaps it wa:
only a question of time before these young Guardsmen (some
even KSU students), worn down by extended duty in a wildcat
strike, worn down by student taunts and missiles, would crack
Operating with loaded weapons and under the absurd policies
which permitted the least of them--in terms of rank--to decid
when to fire, they did decide to fire.  The result was four
dead and nine wounded.  The fault?  It would seem to lay neit
with the young people of the Guard nor the young people they
shot, but rather with the respective leaders of both groups--
because of the communication gap between Guard officials and
university officials and city officials, the communication
gap between university officials and their students, the communication gap between Guard officials and their young troope
The young men who pulled the trigger and their young casualti
had, after all, very little opportunity to discuss the specif

issues of the day.  This may be the most ironic of all the
many communication gaps in this day of the "generation gap."

Although finding the violent actions of students and non-
students during the first three days of May "plainly intoler-
able," the Scranton Commission went on to conclude that only
when the Guard attempted to disperse the Monday rally did
some students react violently.  And, that "The indiscriminate
firing of rifles into a crowd of students and the deaths that
followed were unnecessary, unwarranted, and inexcusable."[22]
For many young people, these unnecessary, unwarranted and
inexcusable killings signalled that President Nixon had
opened up a Second Front.

Our interest here shifts to *what* our subjects knew (and
*how*) at the time of the Monday noon rally.  The Commons, as
noted before, is central to the campus.  The student union,
residence halls and classroom buildings stand on its perimeter.
It would be necessary for many to go out of their way to avoid
the Commons at noon, what with classes beginning and ending,
and meals being served at residence halls and the student
union.

The academic-chain-of-command did not function effectively.
The Provost (Vice President for Academic Affairs) was ill (and
ill-informed); his Associate Provost was in California attending a convention.  The Dean of Education was in Europe, the
Dean of Business Administration was also in California.  The
remaining deans received no official word about the crucial
issues.  And so forth for chairmen and faculty.

As far as we could determine, prior to the assembly only
two methods were used to communicate to the university

community that assembly was prohibited--and there was only
one person who was concerned that these methods might prove
to be inadequate.  Ironically, the one person we can identify
as being concerned about communication was not a university
official, but Major John Simons, chaplain of the 107th Armored
Cavalry Regiment.  When General Canterbury returned at 11:30
to Guard headquarters from his morning meeting, Major Simons
"expressed concern that the students might be unaware that
the noon rally had been prohibited."  He later said that a
campus official told him that the university radio station
would "spread the word."[23]  The station, not realizing the
significance of the message, first presented it at noon on
Sunday and "repeated it several times" after that.  As an
official associated with WKSU told us later, "we were not very
effective nor as clear as we should have been for the information was incorporated into news casts rather than as special
announcements."  This was, he added, "a point of chagrin"
with him and the station.

As for the second method of communicating the prohibition
of assembly--the "special message to the University community
from Matson and Frisina--it was almost totally ineffective.
Of our sample of 417 interviewees, *only sixteen* reported that
it was their original source of such information.  This included not a single faculty member.  Neither of these methods
could reach the commuting student nor the resident student
who was out of town for the weekend; many of these students,
as we saw earlier, came to campus on Monday completely ignorant of the facts.

Many of our student interviewees easily explained the

ineffectiveness of the leaflet.   It is not customary to check
one's residence hall mailbox on either Sunday evening or
Monday morning.   One co-ed told us that she found the "special
message" in her mailbox "after a couple of students had been
shot."   One young man, upon being asked when he first learned
of the prohibition of assembly, simply said:   "I knew after
I was in one!"   Another student said, "When the Guard started
shooting I figured they didn't like the assembly."

Many students reported that they first learned of the
prohibition when the university police and Guard, via bullhorns,
ordered them to disperse, but some later claimed that even
these orders were unintelligible to them.   That the President
had failed to prepare them for this announcement, that he
failed to appear at the rally, that he failed to "legitimize"
the Guard's orders, in our judgment, contributed to the meta-
morphosis of what had been a peaceful, almost playful rally
into a fatal confrontation.

One student told us that he went to the rally without
knowledge of any plans, without even expectations of what
might happen.   He was "angry at President Nixon, Governor
Rhodes and President White.   And Mayor Daley."   Angered by the
Guard's orders, he threw back at the Guard three tear gas
canisters and "perhaps" some rocks, although he could not be
sure.   "It was anarchy," he said.

Thus, Major Simons' fear was unhappily confirmed by our
research.   We feel that the responsibility for communicating
lay clearly with the university administration, and that they
failed to meet that responsibility.   As one dean told us,
"To conduct classes but fail to disseminate information

prohibiting the assembly is stupidity approaching culpability. At best, we can excuse their behavior by ignorance; ignorance of two of the most basic principles of organizational communication:  (1) the relative ineffectiveness of written communication, and (2) the well-established need, particularly in *life and death* matters, for *redundancy*.[24]  A redundancy of media and a redundancy of information are essential.

The "We-wash-our-hands" syndrome manifested by the administration once the Guard came onto campus contributed to this communication failure.  One academic dean who was outspoken in his criticism of the administration's handling of this matter said to us:  "I have a very old-fashioned notion about this--that our responsibility includes trying to save the student's life.  The Big Wheels--White, Matson, Roskens--should have been out there on the Commons, on their hands and knees if necessary, begging the kids and the Guardsmen not to kill each other."

Just what our student subjects knew *before* the noon rally is summarized in Table 5.  (The specific questions can be found in the interview guide included in the Appendix.)  Two conclusions should leap from the table to the reader:  (1) the organizers of the Monday rally were more effective in communicating their plans than was the administration, even with the latter's command of an arsenal of media, in communicating the prohibition of such assemblies (seventy-five percent for the former and only fifty-six percent for the latter); and (2) slightly over thirty percent of the students told us that their behavior would have been different had they been better informed.  The second conclusion is a consequence of the first

KSU CRISIS COMMUNICATION--STUDENTS

| Questions | Yes | ? | No | Did Not Consider | Totals |
|---|---|---|---|---|---|
| Aware rally scheduled for Monday? | 168 | 1 | 56 | | 225 |
| Aware of curfews? | 197 | 0 | 28 | | 225 |
| Aware assembly prohibited? | 126 | 1 | 98 | | 225 |
| Aware live ammo in weapons? | 77 | 19 | 68 | 61 | 225 |
| Behavior different if informed? | 62 | 16 | 147 | | 225 |

TABLE 5

i.e., because the administration failed to communicate the prohibition of assembly, they deprived forty-four percent of our student sample *of the right of decision*.  As a student enrolled in the College of Fine and Professional Arts told us, "I am disturbed at the apparent lack of choice I had in the incident." From all available evidence it appears that at least one of the slain students, Speech student Sandra Scheuer, was between classes, and was attempting to avoid the turmoil when she was shot down in a parking lot not far from the Music and Speech Building.  Perhaps *her* behavior might have been different had she known the facts.

The thirty percent of our sample who said their behavior would have been different had they known the facts is misleading unless one considers that many of those whose behavior would *not* have been different had not attended the rally for various reasons, but six of them even said they would have "felt better" had they been in command of the facts.

Our main point here is that the university had the

responsibility to provide the information by which students could have made an intelligent choice, but it is also of interest to note that of the sixty-two who said they would have behaved differently, forty-three told us they would have exhibited either "flight" or "avoidance" behavior. Of those who said they would have manifested "approach" behavior, eleven would have done so in order to "cool" the situation, and *only* eight students would have approached the rally in order either to participate in a demonstration against the Guard or to protest the handling of the situation.

It is also sad to report that two Vice Presidents told us that they were aware that the Guard had live ammunition in their weapons, but they did not move to communicate this to the university community. Only thirty-four percent of the students were aware of this, some because they assumed it to be so, others because individual Guardsmen had told them.

### KSU CRISIS COMMUNICATION--FACULTY AND CHAIRMEN

| Questions | Yes | ? | No | Did Not Consider | Totals |
|---|---|---|---|---|---|
| Aware rally scheduled for Monday? | 86 | 3 | 60 | | 149 |
| Aware of curfews? | 119 | 0 | 30 | | 149 |
| Aware assembly prohibited? | 66 | 2 | 81 | | 149 |
| Aware live ammo in weapons? | 55 | 7 | 27 | 60 | 149 |
| Behavior different if informed? | 79 | 5 | 65 | | 149 |

TABLE 6

The conclusions reached about student knowledge at the time of the Monday rally can be repeated for faculty and chairmen, as can be seen in Table 6.  If anything, the faculty and chairmen were less well informed than the students.  Only fifty-eight percent knew a rally was scheduled for noon (seventy-five percent for students).  Only forty-four percent were aware that the rally had been prohibited (fifty-six percent for students).  Thirty-seven percent (thirty-four percent for students) were aware that the Guard had live ammunition in their weapons.

Perhaps most significant is the fact that fifty-three percent of the faculty and chairmen said they would have behaved differently had they known the facts.  Seventy-three of the seventy-nine who so responded said they would have used all of their influence--in the classroom and out--either to dissuade the students from confronting the Guard or to attempt to "cool" the situation.  Many of them expressed feelings of guilt and helplessness in connection with this; our inverviewers reported that some of the interviewees showed emotion in responding to this question.  On this matter we can only conclude that in failing to keep the chairmen and faculty apprised of the facts during the crisis, the university administration *failed to employ its greatest resource* during this period. Many of our student subjects reported having turned to their professors for information.  One typical remark was, "Why wasn't the faculty more aware?"  Still others assumed that the faculty was well informed, but chose to remain silent.  As one of these students complained, "The profs should have talked about it more."

Looking at the crisis period from a communication point of view, we can conclude that Kent State University suffered a total breakdown during those days in May. In addition to the internal breakdown, *vital external interfaces* with the city, county and state had not been established. The causes seem to include poor upward-directed communication ("intelligence"-gathering), an absence of planned emergency systems, an "invisible" President, an absence of clearly defined line of authority, broken promises, and, perhaps because of the "We-wash-our-hands" syndrome, an unwillingness to communicate life and death information to the university community. In addition, of course, is Huffman's fatal misinterpretation of Governor Rhodes' remarks at the Sunday news conference.

## The Aftermath

It is difficult to describe the chaotic conditions during and after the killings without imposing an order on events where there had been none. Immediately after the shootings, the prevailing reactions were shock and hysteria.

Upon being notified of the shooting, President White returned from the local restaurant to the campus and declared the university closed. Ronald Kane, youthful County Prosecutor (and a KSU alumnus) learned of the incident over the radio and secured an injunction from Common Pleas Court Judge Albert Caris.

The injunction prohibited students, faculty and administration from entering the campus. This was probably the first time in American history such legal action had been taken, but the university decided not to challenge the injunction.

Concerned parents and friends began to telephone the
university as news reports first began to filter out.  Hoping
to avoid a complete breakdown, the university activated an
emergency procedure which made inoperative all telephones
except a list previously designated.  Unfortunately, the list
had not been revised for five years; because of the high turn-
over during that period many people who should have had functional phones did not--and vice versa.

One man was able to get through to the university by
radio through the Ohio Turnpike Authority.  "They told me it
was all rumor," said Arthur Krause.  "Just a couple of kids
wounded."[25]  His daughter Allison had, of course, been killed.
Her short life and inexcusable death inspired a poem by the
Russian poet, Yevtushenko.

One department chairman was halfway through his lunch
at a nearby pancake house.  "Some guy ran in and said that
two National Guardsmen had been killed.  One of the wait-
resses said, 'They should have shot a dozen students.'"

A Vice President of the university told one of the
academic deans that 500 Black Panthers were "on the way" to
destroy the campus.  A sound truck traversed the campus,
advising students that they would have to leave the university
immediately.  Gathering up from their dorm rooms whatever
belongings they could carry, the students began the evacuation.
The inoperative telephones caused anxiety for students and
their parents.  One student told us, "I couldn't get contact
with the university or call home.  No one had any information.
Some students whose folks live in Florida had to leave the
campus with no place to go."  One chairman described with

some emotion how he had seen students walking along the highways leading out of town carrying bags, dragging clothes--
and weeping.  He took six of them in his car to a local motel
where they could call friends and relatives.  The two authors
decided also to depart Kent for the home of friends out of
town.  They were stopped at a police roadblock and observed
officers "shaking down" long-haired young people who had been
ordered to lean against their car.  The students' cars were
also searched.  It was a miracle that no one was killed in th
instantaneous exodus.

The President of the KSU Board of Trustees, Robert C.
Dix, has a monopoly on the commercial communication media in
Kent by virtue of his ownership of the town's only newspaper,
the *Record-Courier*, and its only commercial radio station,
WKNT.  Immediately after the shootings, his radio station
carried the report that two Guardsmen had been killed by
snipers.  Seven thousand copies of his newspaper carried head
lines with the same message.  Part of the community's subse-
quent and violently anti-university reaction was no doubt due
to this shoddy reporting.  The Myth of the Snipers has been
difficult to kill to this day--even with FBI conclusions to
the contrary.  The Sniper Myth was also used for some time by
Guard leaders to justify the shootings--even though they have
never been able to produce evidence in support of their
allegations.

Although it was probably written before the shootings, t
May Fourth issue of the *Record-Courier* also carried a signed
editorial by President Dix in which he said, "Its a good thin
the Guard was nearby, mobilized and ready to fight."

For weeks to come pages of the *Record-Courier* were filled with letters to the editor, mainly in support of the Guard. Many expressed rage, even hatred, toward the faculty and students.  A petition commending the Guard was circulated and signed by thousands of local citizens.  Rumors of citizens' vigilante groups circulated on campus.  The Kent City Council attempted to solve the community's problems by providing a referendum on measures designed to ban live entertainment and alcoholic beverages.  Although these expressions were shocking to most members of the academic community, they were no doubt useful as a catharsis.

The father of one of the slain students is a Jew who fled Nazi Germany.  Martin Scheuer, father of Sandy Scheuer, suffered the insult of having one of his city councilmen in Boardman, Ohio, publicly announce, "I think instead of four people getting shot down, if 4004 got shot down a lot  of this would stop."[26]

And at least one student told us of seeing Middle America's reply to the two-finger peace symbol.  Four fingers were flashed and followed by the formation of a "zero" by the thumb and index finger of the same hand.  This signified the score:  "Guard--four, students--nothing."

The university's sixtieth birthday--May 10, 1970--passed quietly without students on the campus.  A Kent State University-in-exile was established at Case Western Reserve University in Cleveland and another in Oberlin.  Who knows how many colleges and universities were closed in sympathy for Kent State?  But during this period when students were enjoined from entering their own campus, Kent State University had its finest hour.  The remaining weeks of spring quarter's classe

were conducted in churches, in professors' homes, by telepho

and by correspondence.  There was generated a closeness, a

personalization of education that neither teachers nor stude

had experienced before.  Grading procedures were liberalizee

Oral examinations for advanced degrees were conducted in hor

and instead of the usual bureaucratic forms in quintuplicate

a hand scrawled note to the effect that a student had met th

requirements of his degree was sufficient.  "We had," said

one dean, "an orgy of flexibility and humaneness."

Then came the onslaught of investigations.  The FBI, th

Scranton Commission, the state, the county and, of course,

the university with its multitudinous commissions and commit

tees all began their investigations.  The County Attorney

later displayed the contraband gathered during the ransacki

of the rooms of KSU's thirty-one dormitories, housing almost

8,000 students.  As one newspaper summarized the results:

> They included two typical hunting weapons, a .22
> caliber rifle and a shotgun; about 60 knives; three
> slingshots and several BB guns.

> The police, who had no search warrant, also
> confiscated several hashish pipes, six growing
> marijuana plants and a yellow button saying,
> "Dare to Struggle, Dare to Win."[27]

A middle-aged businessman was heard to say in a downtow

coffee shop, "You could have collected more than that at my

fraternity house when I was in college--and there wasn't a

revolutionary in the bunch."

The university denied that its security forces had par

ticipated in the search, but one of their officers was late

suspended when he was charged with stealing money from a

student's room during the search.

Prosecutor Kane announced that he would require financial aid from the state in conducting a Grand Jury investigation because of the wide scope of the case. The state responded by conducting its own Grand Jury, before which Governor Rhodes did not testify. After hearing over 300 witnesses, the Grand Jury presented on October 16, 1970, thirty "true bills" covering twenty-five defendants. All defendants were connected with the university including Craig Morgan, Student Body President. The Grand Jury found that "those members of the National Guard who were present on the hill adjacent to Taylor Hall on May 4, 1970, fired their weapons in the honest and sincere belief and under circumstances which would have logically caused them to believe that they would suffer serious bodily injury had they not done so. They are not, therefore, subject to criminal prosecution under the laws of this state for any death or injury resulting therefrom."

Perhaps not surprisingly, the state exonerated the state. There is some doubt, however, about the degree to which the direction of the Grand Jury was impartial. One of those appointed by the state to direct the Grand Jury was the chairman of the Portage County Republican executive committee, Seabury Ford. Mr. Ford was quoted after the Grand Jury report was issued as saying that the Guardsmen should have "shot all the troublemakers." When it was revealed that Ford had once served with the 107th Cavalry of the ONG, whose Troop G was among the Guardsmen who fired at the students on May 4, even Ohio Attorney General Paul W. Brown admitted that had he known of this association he would have "avoided appointing" Ford to help direct the investigation.[28]

After considering the evidence, the Grand Jury conclude
that the events of Friday, May 1 "constituted a riot"; that
the events of Saturday, May 2 "constituted a riot"; that the
events of Sunday, May 3 "constituted a riot"; but that the
assembly at noon on Monday, May 4, *did not constitute a riot*
The Jury concluded about that gathering:

> The gathering on the Commons on May 4, 1970, was
> in violation of the directive of May 3rd, issued by
> the University Vice President in charge of Student
> Affairs. We find that all the persons assembled were
> ordered to disperse on numerous occasions, but failed
> to do so. Those orders, given by a Kent State Uni-
> versity policeman, caused a violent reaction and the
> gathering quickly degenerated into a riotous mob.
> It is obvious that if the order to disperse had been
> heeded, there would not have been the consequences of
> that fateful day. Those who acted as participants
> and agitators are guilty of deliberate, criminal
> conduct. Those who were present as cheerleaders and
> onlookers, while not liable for criminal acts, must
> morally assume a part of the responsibility for what
> occurred.

Several important points are established by this para-
graph. First, the assembly itself was not a riot. Second,
the assembly became "riotous" only when attempts were made to
disperse the gathering. Third, *the only justification for
the attempt to disperse the gathering was the Matson-Frisina
directive of May 3*. We can be sure that if the Grand Jury
had been able to find additional means by which to justify
the dispersal, it would have been included in its report.
Thus, we find full support for our interpretation that the
"impression" formed by university attorney John Huffman from
a conversation with a Guard officer produced the document
which, in turn, was the major, if not the sole factor in
forcing the fatal dispersal attempt.

Perhaps the best way to conclude our summary of the aftermath is with the student point of view.  One hoped for some evidence that the profound, structural and attitudinal changes called for by the university's commissions and committees had begun to be implemented.  More than eight months after the killings, however, the following editorial entitled "Silence," appeared in the student newspaper.

> There is a very quiet mood on campus this quarter. People are simply being and not doing.
>
> Students appear worn out from the tension of the fall quarter and the after-effects of the spring are now a dying ember.
>
> Students seem more methodical, perhaps more studious, but are doing less questioning, less looking for the changes called for during the last eight months.
>
> Everyone is simply tired of hassles.
>
> Perhaps now we can get together and talk.
>
> There's so much to answer.
>
> Administrators, however, seem to have withdrawn into their shells.  Reporters have found that questions are not answered or are simply ignored.
>
> *FYI*, the administration's own newspaper, had no mention of any administration viewpoint on anything. Editor Paul Schlemmer said he wanted to make it more student-oriented.
>
> We have a student paper.  We understood that *FYI* was to represent the administrative viewpoint.
>
> Then maybe we'll never know what the administration thinks.
> . . . . . . . . . . . . . . . . . . . . . . . . . . . . . . . . . . . . . . . . . . . . . . . . . .
>
> Silence will only enable administrators to bury future questions.
>
> Silence, however, has left blood in its wake in the past.  *FYI* was started to answer questions and it, too, as memory fades, is having less and less to say.
>
> And the quiet that helped precipitate past problems has fallen again, like a heavy curtain.

We must talk; we must communicate.

Administrators must give answers--students have th
right to know.

Isn't that what a university is all about--communi
cation?

Why wait for another spring to start talking
again?[29]

*References*

1. Our source for the first fifty years of KSU is Phillip R. Shriver's,
   *The Years of Youth: Kent State University, 1910-1960*, Kent State
   University Press, 1960.

2. *Ibid.*, p. 84.

3. *Ibid.*

4. *Ibid.*, p. 168.

5. *Ibid.*, p. 129.

6. *Ibid.*, p. 185.

7. *Summary of Kent State University Study*, R. H. Goettler and Associate
   October 1, 1969, p. 15.

8. *Ibid.*

9. *Ibid.*, p. 18.

10. *Ibid.*, p. 21.

11. *Ibid.*, p. 16.

12. *Special Report: The Kent State Tragedy*, The President's Commission
    on Campus Unrest, p. 16 (1970).

13. *Ibid.*, p. 17.

14. *Ibid.*, p. 27.

15. *Ibid.*, p. 31.

16. *Ibid.*

17. Shriver, p. 111.

18. *Special Report: The Kent State Tragedy*, The President's Commission
    on Campus Unrest, p. 38 (1970).

19. *Ibid.*

20. *Ibid.*, pp. 38-39.

21. *Ibid.*, p. 42.

22. *Ibid.*, p. 90.

23. *Ibid.*, pp. 47-48.

24. See, for example, Thomas L. Dahle, "An Objective and Comparative Study of Five Methods of Transmitting Information to Business and Industrial Employees," *Speech Monographs*, 21, pp. 21-28.

25. *Akron Beacon Journal*, May 24, 1970, p. A23.

26. *Akron Beacon Journal*, January 3, 1971, p. D9.

27. *Akron Beacon Journal*, May 24, 1970, p. A24.

28. *Record-Courier*, October 29, 1970, p. 1.

29. *Daily Kent Stater*, January 12, 1971, p. 4.

CHAPTER TWO:   THE ADMINISTRATION AND THE DEANS

"The first executive function," wrote Chester Barnard in
his classic book on management, "is to develop and maintain a
system of communication."[1]  For Barnard, communication was
far more than bulletins, house organs, suggestion systems and
telephone information centers.  For him, a successful executive
as well as theorist, there could be no *organization* until the
executive had assured that members were able to communicate
with each other.  He took a "systems" view of communication--
that each part of the organization is related to every other
part.  Thus, communication is the very structure of organization, giving the executive such responsibilities as placing
effective communicators in key positions.  In short, he must
establish and maintain a system of communication which permits
the easy upward flow of information to benefit decision-
making, the easy downward flow of information to benefit the
implementation of policy, the easy horizontal flow of information to benefit coordination and the easy flow of information
in all directions to facilitate the functional interdependence
of all parts of the organization.  It is an ecological view
of human organization.

Two conclusions are quite clear as we move from crisis
communication to the day-to-day operations of Kent State University:  (1) the chief executive, the President, has failed
in his first function of establishing and maintaining a system

of communication; and (2) the breakdown of communication dur
the crisis could have been predicted from the problems and
weaknesses of the day-to-day "system" of communication.

At every level of the university we encountered the com
plaint that the President was not sufficiently visible, not
sufficiently accessible. This criticism took two forms:  (1
that he did not realize the symbolic importance of his commu
cation role within the university; and (2) that the Presiden
did not make himself sufficiently available for face-to-face
communication.

In regard to the first complaint, examples would be tha
President White should have appeared at the Monday rally, th
he should have appeared at the May Fifth faculty meeting hel
in an Akron church, and that when he was allowed by law to
reply to the Grand Jury charges that he should have done so
on campus, speaking to the university community, rather than
limiting himself to speeches in Washington, D. C., and Cleve
land. As one member of his cabinet (the four Vice President
his Executive Assistant and another Assistant for Planning
and Analysis) put it, President White "does not appreciate
the meaningfulness of his appearance." And another said, "W
must find a way of relieving him of his burdens so that he c
get out and about--into the general community as well as the
university community."

The second complaint--that the President did not make
himself sufficiently available for face-to-face communicatio
is far more serious and one which is almost entirely of the
President's making. We must approach this problem by first
acknowledging that it is a complaint heard in almost all lar

and complex organizations (although not with the volume and the intensity it was heard at KSU); it is mathematically impossible for one man to maintain one-to-one communication with every member of an organization. For example, as the number of people in a group increases, the potential number of channels of interaction increases geometrically--the basis for the well known "span of control" limiting the number of subordinates one person can supervise.

Nonetheless, this problem was exacerbated at KSU by the President's indecisiveness. And indicated in the previous chapter, the emergency chain-of-authority was established, according to one Vice President, because of the President's inability to make a decision. One Associate Professor who described himself as "aggressive and knowledgeable," said, "The President feels that a decision delayed is a decision well handled." And, presumably, a decision never made is a decision best handled.

A closely related problem is the widespread concern that the President had delegated insufficient authority to the four Vice Presidents, that he devoted too much time to decisions better handled by those closer to the problem. As one Vice President put it, "The four of us have an in-group joke; we refer to ourselves not as the four Vice Presidents, but as four assistants to the President." As another cabinet member put it, "The President's visibility has dwindled. Candidly, this could be alleviated if he chose to delegate. He chooses instead to operate by 'blue note'; the dictation discs flow steadily out of that office."

The impact of this lack of delegation was two-fold:    (1)

his attention to detail stole invaluable time from both
symbolic communication and the attending to larger problems;
and (2) it forced an even greater need on the "middle management" of the university to see the President on relatively
insignificant issues.  To repeat, the lack of delegation
robbed the President's limited time-available-for-communicati
and further compressed that time by creating a greater need
for his availability.  One source extremely close to members
of the Board of Trustees told us that the Board had long
realized this problem, and had tried subtly to encourage a
change in "style."  Three hypotheses were advanced by cabinet
members to explain this problem:  (1) he lacked trust in the
competency of his administrators; (2) it was just the way he
worked, his "style"; and (3) the "President has seen things
not done right in the past and would rather *do* than *undo*."
None of these is excusable.  If the problem was a matter of
personal style, he was the wrong man for the job.  If it were
either the first or the third explanation, it is clear that
he should have replaced the administrators he could not trust
each of whom was originally appointed to the job by President
White.

The cabinet itself did not seem to function as intended.
One member felt that its function was to make decisions by
"consensus," but the other members feel that it was not a
decision-making body.  As one member put it, "The agenda is
defined by the President.  The informal give-and-take we need
so much does not happen until we have a yellow light situatic
This makes for another one of our biggest problems--an insufficient flow of information between the major divisions of th

university at the Vice Presidential level."  Even in those
rare cases where a good give-and-take did take place, no vote
was taken and the decision was later made by the President.
This fact had been learned by many aggressive individuals at
every level of the university.  Hence, those who anticipate
an important decision, including students, want to see "The
Man," and preferably be the last person to see him before he
made his decision.

Several members of the cabinet asserted that much academic
business was brought to the cabinet by the President which, as
one member put it, "I would take to the deans."  The deans
agreed.  There was almost unanimous opinion that administrative
decision-making suffered from an inadequate input from the
academic sector.  Only one member of the cabinet, the Vice
President (and Provost) for Academic Affairs, was viewed as
a representative of academic interests.  It was asserted about
the "non-academic" Vice Presidents--and admitted by them in
at least two cases--that they were relatively isolated from
faculty and students.  Even those deans who realized that the
cabinet did not take votes feared that the "weight of argument"
always originated from non-academic sources.  In addition, eight
of the nine academic deans reported to us that the President
was unavailable to them either collectively or individually.
In fairness it should be noted that the President tried to
rely heavily on the Faculty Senate, but as we shall see later,
that body was viewed by the deans and the faculty alike as
being unrepresentative of academic views.  Finally, when one
realizes that the administration had admittedly listened to
a biased sample of students ("only to the ones they view as the

'good' guys," as one dean put it), it must be clear that the
academic input available to the President was grossly inadequate.  The communication between the President and the academic sector can be characterized by a preoccupation with
transmission-oriented, downward-directed systems as opposed t
concern with *two-way systems*.

### The Academic Officers

The outstanding communication problem facing the academi
officers of the various colleges (Education, Arts and Science
Fine and Professional Arts, Business Administration, Health
and Physical Education, Library Science, Graduate School,
Honors College and Nursing) was mentioned above.  At least
eight of the nine deans would have agreed with this statement
made by the dean of one of the larger colleges:  "The top
administration is not informed in depth on the needs and wel-
fare of the academic programs--the heart of the institution.
This is not the fault of the Academic Vice President, nor of
the previous one, because we [the deans] are reasonably sure
he communicates our wishes and requests, but we have looked a
the cabinet and the long range planning committee, and we wor
about the under-representation of the academic area.  Further
more, we feel that different decisions may have been made wit
better communication."

The same problem as viewed by seven other deans was
expressed in the following manner:

> [1]  The President and Vice Presidents fear face-to
> face communication except in the cabinet.  They depend o
> the written medium--*FYI*, bulletins and confidential memo
> There is only one academic member of the cabinet and the
> weight of argument is always against us.

[2]  There is a lack of response to specific questions. My correspondence is not answered by the President.

[3]  He [President White] has never responded to me. He has never answered me. Even on a university-wide problem not out of channels. His advisors are, except for the Provost, all non-academic people. The prominence given to them inflates their self-importance and deflates that of the Provost.

[4]  As a group we [the deans] feel blocked out of the action. We advise the Provost but he is the only academic man on the cabinet. Those other men are isolated from faculty and students. Therefore, the President is isolated from the faculty and students. He doesn't think so, but I do absolutely. His meetings at home with students and the Executive Committee of the Faculty Senate are admirable, but the students are not typical and the meetings take place in a polite social atmosphere. The Faculty Senate is not reputable with the faculty, its Executive Committee even less so. The President has consistently resisted our attempts to meet with him. He tries to do too much of the work. Lou [Provost Louis Harris] does not feel free to make decisions, particularly on budget matters.

[5]  I have saved every communication from the President's office for four years. It will curl your hair. It takes up a small file cabinet. Most of them have a "Confidential" imprimatur, so I can't discuss them with anyone else. But the greater problem is the correspondence he ignores. I have copies of twenty-four unanswered memos sent to the President about university-wide problems.

[6]  The academic segment is seriously underrepresented at the cabinet level. The President does see the Faculty Senate and some students. We deans have repeatedly expressed our need to see him, but he does not respond. The deans and the department chairmen are the uneasiest people in the university. We have overcentralization in the President even with a sizable administrative bureaucracy. *FYI* sometimes has useful information, but the faculty gets it before I do. For example, I didn't know about the injunction against entering the campus and was ejected from my office by the campus police.

[7]  The cabinet has too little input provided by academic people. White has surrounded himself with non-academic, non-intellectual, perhaps anti-intellectual people who manifest an absence of humaneness and comprehension of academic life. White chose them from the College of Education and then he chose to grow. Now this overgrown place is run by the legates of the Normal School.

President White offered to the deans the explanation that

he operated in such a matter because he did not wish to unde
cut the authority of the Provost.  The deans, however, felt
that the Provost's authority in reality had already been und
cut by the insufficient delegation.  As quoted above, one de
said:  "His advisors are, except for the Provost, all non-
academic people.  The prominence given to them inflates thei
self-importance and deflates that of the Provost."  As anoth
dean said:  "He deals with *every* faculty contract.  He has
even changed some, by $200 or $300 without reason.  The 'con
fidential' memos circumscribe and downgrade the Provost.  Th
Provost is not backed.  The President simply has not grasped
the idea of delegation."  Another dean said:  "Almost everything has to go across the President's desk.  I heard one of
my fellow deans say to him, 'You shouldn't have to waste you
time on this.'"

The recommendations the deans proposed for these proble
during our interviews seem reasonable and logical.  They included:  (1) increased delegation to the Provost; (2) increa
academic representation on the cabinet; and (3) regularly
scheduled meetings with the deans.  Most, however, were skep
that they would be accepted by the President because, as one
dean put it, "We have troubled to point [these] things out
before."  Sadly enough, a significant communication blockage
at any level of an organization has ramifications for other
levels.  "Our relations with students are affected," said on
dean, "by our ignorance of decisions made by the administration.  We need to know, but we [deans and chairmen] are the
forgotten channels."

It would seem appropriate to return at this point to the

pair of theses posed at the beginning of this chapter as we passed from crisis communication to day-to-day operations of the university:  "(1) the chief executive, the President, has failed in his first function of establishing and maintaining a system of communication; and (2) the breakdown of communication during the crisis could have been predicted from the problems and weaknesses of the day-to-day 'system' of communication."

That President White failed on the first point cannot be denied.  Isolated from and unwilling to communicate with his academic officers, no "system" can be said to have existed. Isolated from the decision-center (President White), the deans were crippled in their dealings with chairmen, faculty and students.  The question of whether a system had ever been established is a moot question.  Those who were in a position to observe President White function as Vice President and as Dean of Education were split.  Some felt that his later "style" was evident in those positions.  Others felt not, but one source who had served on the Search Committee which selected White to replace retiring President Bowman told us that the committee's greatest reservation about candidate White had been his "lack of communicative ability."  Regardless of the answer to this question, it seems quite clear that even if President White had once established a system of communication, a system designed for a university of 12,000 students is not adequate for a university of 20,000 plus.  Those in a position to observe, by virtue of long tenure, repeatedly told us that the most significant if not the only structural change made during White's administration was to create three additional Vice-Presidents

and to permit the rapid expansion of a large administrative
bureaucracy under each of these new positions.  Faculty bulletins, such as *FYI* and telephone information centers, although
useful media, cannot be substitutes for a *structural system*
of communication.[2]

The second point, that the problems of crisis communication could have been predicted from the day-to-day operations
of the university, seems also well established.  The inability
to delegate authority, particularly to the Provost, was appare
in both cases.  Almost a month after the crisis, one dean
said:  "I didn't know who was in charge during the crisis.  I
*still* don't know who was in charge.  The Provost should have
been."  Isolated from the academic chain-of-authority during
routine operations, the President also failed to activate that
system during the crisis--leaving the deans, chairmen, faculty
and students to inform themselves.  "We just weren't plugged
in then and we aren't now," a dean told us.

Other communication problems faced by the deans were less
serious than those mentioned above, but which were nonetheless
demoralizing:  a non-responsive Maintenance office (but one
dean argued that maintenance represented more a question of
*technical* competence than communicative competency) and other
offices such as Admissions and Registration whose decisions
have a great impact on academic programs.  In the case of
Housing, Parking, Traffic and Security offices, they were seen
as making important decisions with neither consultation nor
consideration of the faculty.  One dean detailed a case which
would be "traceable" in these pages, and then concluded:
"Once these decisions are made, there is no way to find out

who made them.  Thus, they are irreversible."

Inherent to these problems seems to be a perceived goal-displacement.  The non-academic or service offices forgot that they provide the *means* to the mission of the organization: teaching and learning.  Instead, they gave the impression that their services and regulations are ends in themselves, understood only by themselves.

The deans did identify two additional problems of great importance.  The first was the bifurcation of Student Affairs and Academic Affairs--with very little communication between the two divisions.  "We deal with the student as Academic Man, they [Student Affairs] deal with him as Social Man; nobody deals with him Man-to-Man."  (One department chairman referred to this same problem, saying that no one deals with the Total student--"but I am not," he adamantly added, "suggesting that we create a new Vice President For the Total Student!")

Some of the deans reported losing rapport with students for having sent them to Student Affairs for the "run-around," but several were willing to admit that they had done less to correct this than had the Student Affairs office.  That is, Student Affairs had made a greater attempt to communicate with the academic sector than vice versa.

The deans' suggestions for improving this situation include the following:  the complete absorption of the Student Affairs personnel and function into the academic sector; regular attendance of the Vice President for Student Affairs at Faculty Senate meetings; and the locating of Student Affairs counselors in collegial and departmental offices.

Perhaps the most withering criticism offered by the deans

focused on professor-student communication. "The faculty does not do its job well," said one dean. "We all know about the instructors at the freshmen level who play games inside the classroom and can't be reached outside the classroom." A dean reported that his own son, a KSU student, had to buy mimeographed lectures from an instructor, and that the faculty "show their contempt for students by indifference to their responsibilities to the student."

Academic advising was a "grave weakness" according to one dean. The faculty was "notorious," said another dean, for its poor advising. They were "unavailable, not even in during office hours." One dean felt that the undergraduate had been "sacrificed" to rapidly expanded graduate program. At least one dean acknowledged that fault did not all lay with the faculty. He asserted that it was impossible to get information out of the computers and to the advisor, information which is crucial to intelligent advising. Other deans felt that excellence in advising had not been rewarded.

There was also the widespread feeling among the deans that students did not have the opportunity to provide inputs for departmental decisions; they expressed, in general, support for the increased involvement in departmental affairs and support for the idea of an All-University Senate, a policy-making body including administrators, students and faculty.

It is clear that the academic officers were also beginning to question two cherished values of KSU. The first is tenure; two deans told us that this concept requires rethinking because it protects incompetents and student-haters. Three spoke to us of their fear that KSU had grown too large. One suggested the "radical restructuring" of the university into a "cluster of small, autonomous colleges with centralized support serving all of them." Another proposed a similar cluster concept, but favored their being "self-contained, handling everything but dormitories."

To summarize the communication relations of the university administration and the deans, we can say that it was almost non-existent--before, during and after the crisis. Indeed, the breakdown between the administration and the academic sector--deans, chairmen, faculty and students--during the crisis was not atypical. It was simply more dramatic than was the case with mundane, day-to-day issues.

### References

1. Chester I. Barnard, *The Functions of the Executive*, Harvard University Press, Cambridge, p. 226 (1938).

2. For the effect of increased size on organization and communication, see Paul E. Mott, *The Organization of Society*, Prentice-Hall, Inc., Englewood Cliffs, New Jersey, pp. 48-70 (1965).

CHAPTER THREE:  DEPARTMENT CHAIRMEN

The basic unit of Kent State University, like any university, is of course the *academic department*. We shall use
that term even though at KSU they are variously called departments, schools and instructional units. We use the term to
apply to any unit reporting directly to an academic dean, and
for the most part, representing an academic discipline.  It
is basic because it is the irreducible community of scholars.
It is the one academic unit with which the student identifies.
The question, "What's your major?" serves as a ritual for
students who are strangers, and the answer gives clues about
how they might relate.

The department, like the university, is under attack.
As Warren Bennis, a student of organization with experience
as a university administrator, said:  "Unless departments
learn how to adapt, become more responsive to students on the
one hand and the changes in society on the other, 'departmentalitis' will prevent many universities from adapting--
and innovating--in any basic sense.  The university is harder
to reorganize than a cemetary."[1]

We shall take a close look at KSU's "departmentalitis,"
looking through the eyes of chairmen, faculty and students.
Of the twenty-nine chairmen we were able to interview, twenty
(or sixty-nine percent) identified some kind of problem at
the cabinet level similar to those raised by the deans.

"Does President White really exist?" a chairman in Arts and Sciences asked us. Another chairman in the same college said: "The faculty never see the President. We have to deal with people we don't know. Matson [Vice President for Student Affairs] and White are isolated, and the Provost is frozen out of decision-making." The chairman of one of KSU's largest departments told us that in the process of securing a government grant of nearly one half million dollars, he spent one and one-half weeks of "frustration and rage" in an unsuccessful attempt to get President White's signature. At the last moment he had to crash a formal dance to secure the signature.

A chairman of a social science department argued that it is the President's function to "encourage and insist that channels be open," but that President White "has no channels with the faculty--no organization--and messages from *ad hoc* groups perish without response. The model here is communication only through legitimate bodies even though we are a 'legit' body without a channel." Another chairman said, "We [chairmen] can't communicate with the President and this is coupled with insufficient delegation. There is a studied effort to make us stick to the chain of command, but the President himself doesn't observe it--he picks up the phone and calls faculty members in my department without going through me."

The delay on decisions vital to departmental functioning was a typical complaint. "Do they [the administration] hope to kill a request by a long delay?" asked one suspicious chairman. The chairmen tend to see this as taking place "above the dean," as one chairman said. As a chairman in the College

of Fine and Professional Arts put it, "There is a delay at the
Provost's level because he has no authority to decide and no
access to the President.  Communication has come to a stand-
still with us and this affects what we can say to our faculty."
Another chairman complained that on a matter crucial to his
department he tried to see the President and was denied access
and even an appointment by President White's secretary.  "It
is impossible to reach him," he continued.  He then asked the
interviewer, "Does anyone reach him?"

Several of the chairmen were still angry at the time of
the interviews because of the President's handling of the
crisis.  "The President," said one chairman, "failed to get
to the chairmen at the height of the crisis and the period
following."  "He should have been out there Monday," said one
chairman who *had* been "out there" on Monday, May 4, trying to
cool the situation.  Of those who complained about their dealings with the administration, all but four complained about
the high volume of paper cascading down from the administration into their office.  "We are buried under a huge pile of
paper," complained one chairman.  "You have to read ten documents from the President in order to get one that makes sense,"
complained a long-term chairman.  Another chairman with long
experience told us:  "I've dealt with Bob White as dean,
Vice President and President.  He has always been inaccessible,
has always had his penchant for locking himself up in his
office and writing confidential memos."  Another simply suggested, "It should be possible [for the President] to formulate
a reasonable two-way network."

Like the deans, many of the chairmen felt uneasy that
there is only one "academic guy," as one phrased it, on the
President's cabinet.  Six chairmen complained about a "lack
of openness" in the administration.  The same number of chairmen felt, as one told us, "More faculty people would feel
better about decisions--when made--if they understood the
process involved in making the decision."  "There is a general
feeling," said another chairman, "that we don't know *why*
decisions are made as they are at the cabinet level."

The chairmen were pleased by the President's reliance
upon the Faculty Senate, but those who spoke of this vehicle
were *unanimous* in their judgment that it did not represent
faculty views, particularly its Executive Committee, because
of the high percentage of "pro-administration" members from
the College of Education.

Those few chairmen (nine) who had no complaints about
communication with the administration showed similarities and
differences.  Three of them had been serving for two years or
less in the job of chairman.  They had not yet learned their
job as is clear from one who could identify neither the name
of the three non-academic Vice Presidents nor the division
each headed.  On the other hand, one had over fifteen years in
the job and another nearly twenty-five years in various capac-
ities at KSU.  Both claimed they had developed effective
*informal* channels by which to operate.

Another variable seemed to emerge, one which we neither
anticipated nor measured: *aggressiveness*.  It is interesting
to contrast the comments of non-complaining chairmen such as,
"I deal only with the dean," and, "We are not encouraged when

we go beyond the dean's office," with the behavior of the
chairman who crashed the formal dance to get the President's
signature and the chairman who told us about sitting in the
lobby of the President's office to wait for a chance to button-
hole him when he left his inner office.

A final variable would seem to be professional identification.  President White was once the Dean of the College of
Education, and far fewer and less severe complaints emanated
from its chairmen than from any other college.  It is possible
that the President maintained better communication with his
former college than with others, but there was little evidence
in our interviews to support this hypothesis.  Rather, it
seemed to be a case of professional identification.

A curious phenomenon began to surface in the interviews
with chairmen.  Most of the chairmen who were critical of the
President's communicative ability were emphatic in expressing
their belief in his integrity and character.  Many, in fact,
were apologetic for being critical of his communication
behavior.  "I just came from a paternalistic and autocratic
university," said one new chairman, "and it didn't deserve
to happen here.  Maybe the twentieth century caught up with
us."

No doubt the most convincing evidence on this point came
when the chairmen were asked to list the three *most* and the
three *least* credible or believable sources of information
within the university.  The sources, which do not add up to
eighty-seven because some chairmen either could not or would
not name three, are listed in Table 1.  When one combines the
President as a source with his "office" and "media" (*FYI*, the

*Official Bulletin*, etc.) as sources, he would be the most credible source for slightly more than sixty-two percent of the chairmen. This is in contrast to the sixty-nine percent of the chairmen who were critical of his communication behavio

DEPARTMENT CHAIRMEN'S MOST CREDIBLE SOURCES

President White. . . . . . . . . . . . . . . . . . . . . . . . 10

Presidential Office and Media (*FYI*, etc.). . . . . . . . . . 8

Vice President and Provost Harris. . . . . . . . . . . . . . 10

Dean Harkness (Arts and Sciences). . . . . . . . . . . . . . 9

Associate Provost Hall . . . . . . . . . . . . . . . . . . . 4

Dean Flower (Fine and Professional Arts) . . . . . . . . . . 4

Miscellaneous Sources. . . . . . . . . . . . . . . . . . . . 21

TABLE 1

It seems clear from these data that credibility has little to do with communicative ability in certain situations. In this case, for example, there is no doubt a degree of "routinized" or, to use Aristotle's term, "inartistic" credibility which resides in such an office as President of Kent State University. Such "positional" credibility might be diminished by communications from that office if perceived as lacking in "artistic credibility," i.e., good sense, good character and good will, but this was apparently not the case with President White. His credibility remained relatively high, in spite of or because of his noncommunicative style. It is unfortunate, we must add, that he failed to exploit this credibility during the time of crisis.

The miscellaneous sources, none of which received more

than two votes, include such diverse sources as the student newspaper (*Daily Kent Stater*), the campus radio station (WKSU), Vice President Dunn (Business and Finance), Dean McGrath (Graduate School) and a long list of individuals. *No non-academic source was listed by more than two of the department chairmen as the most credible or believable.* This should heighten the irony that these sources, these resources, were not employed during the crisis.

The chairmen's *dis*trust of non-academic sources can be seen in their list of *least* credible or believable sources within the university presented in Table 2. Although votes

DEPARTMENT CHAIRMEN'S LEAST CREDIBLE SOURCES

Faculty Rumor Mill and Grapevine. . . . . . . . . . . . . . . 6

Vice President Matson (Student Affairs) . . . . . . . . . . . 5

Student Rumor Mill and Grapevine. . . . . . . . . . . . . . 4

Vice President Roskens (Administration) . . . . . . . . . . . 4

*Daily Kent Stater* (student newspaper) . . . . . . . . . . . 3

Campus Police . . . . . . . . . . . . . . . . . . . . . . . 3

Vice President & Provost Harris (Academic Affairs). . . . . . 2

Miscellaneous Sources . . . . . . . . . . . . . . . . . . . .14

TABLE 2

for least credible sources were more diverse than for most credible sources--partly because the chairmen were more reluctant to name the former than the latter--non-academic sources are prominent. Vice Presidents Matson and Roskens are the most frequently mentioned individuals. In addition, only five of the fourteen miscellaneous sources were in the

academic sector of the university.  Although one dean accused
Vice Presidents Matson and Roskens of a "Cleopatra Syndrome"
(defined by the dean as "a tendency to talk only to each other
and to others like them") it would appear that the phenomenon
applies equally to department chairmen--at least if credibility
or believability is a component of the syndrome.

Several chairmen were critical of the (Vice President
for Academic Affairs and) Provost's office for reversing
departmental and collegial recommendations on promotions and
salaries--without informing the college and department of the
decision.  "I read it in the paper," said one chairman.  One
Arts and Science chairman did complain about his dean's propensity to express that he "needs within twenty minutes the
number of faculty members within the department who have
webbed feet."  Generally, however, the chairmen reported that
their communication with deans and the Provost was excellent.

The "departmentalitis" referred to earlier began to
reveal itself at this level.  Most of the chairmen reported
that they rarely saw any fellow chairmen outside their own
college.

The chairmen were in agreement with the deans about the
problem of undergraduate academic advising.  They applied such
terms to advising as "a disgrace," "atrocious," "poor," "bad,"
and "It stinks!"  Why?  The chairman felt that it was because
of a low level of motivation on the part of the faculty.  Most
admitted that there were neither rewards nor sanctions to
dispense on the basis of advising.  Some chairmen were frank
to admit that Kent State University's rapid and underfinanced
expansion into graduate studies during the sixties had forced

them, the chairmen, to rob "Peter" (the undergraduate program) to pay "Paul" (the graduate program).  By this they meant that small graduate seminars and reduced loads for the graduate faculty were achieved only by herding undergraduates into classes of 400 or 500 enrollments, and by decreased availability of the faculty.

Many chairmen felt powerless to deal with the problem of tenure.  Advising is not explicitly included among the four criteria to be applied in considering faculty promotions.  "We have a couple of faculty members," said one chairman, "who don't teach, don't advise and who treat students like buck-ass privates.  Students shouldn't be exposed to professors who hate them, hate teaching and hate advising.  They are not competent, but they have tenure.  And some have outside incomes.  How can you deal with them?"

Tenure was seen to complicate the problem.  Said one chairman:  "There are people who have tenure who aren't competent.  But you can't do anything to them unless you prove moral turpitude.  I have to be a devious operator and make life unpleasant for them."  Another chairman spoke to the problem of tenure in this way:  "The faculty must be protected from a dictatorial administration, but the university and the department must be protected against persons who are not qualified, who don't teach, who don't advise.  We must rethink tenure."

Because of these problems and others, we were surprised to learn from the chairmen about a widespread "quiet revolution" taking place at the departmental level.  In most of the departments engaged in graduate studies the chairmen spoke of

the extreme pressure being applied by students for participation in departmental decision-making. The students were
organizing. Potentially explosive situations existed in at
least six departments. "We were saved by the bell at the end
of spring quarter," said the chairman of one of the involved
departments. Said another, "Expect a flap in our department
next fall." (True to the predictions, the "quiet revolution"
became rather noisy during the fall quarter, requiring external intervention to quiet them in at least two cases.)

"The pressure is on from the graduate students," said the
chairman of one of KSU's larger departments. "They want more
than committee membership. They want to be in on faculty
promotions and faculty recruiting. I'd like to see it, but
the deadheads don't." The same chairman went on to point out
that with such large numbers of students, there was no way to
know the grievances of the majority unless they did organize
in some way to express them.

A pattern seemed to be discernible. In most departments
the faculty was found to be deeply involved in departmental
decision-making (although this was not universal--several
autocratic chairmen were operating with almost total power).
In such cases, the graduate students organized and pressed
for participation. The faculty of the department then tended
to polarize. To oversimplify somewhat, the senior faculty
tended to resist while the junior faculty supported the students. The faculty battle over the issue has tended to be the
most intense part of the pattern, the crisis. Attempts to
topple a chairman were even made, but generally a compromise
was engineered which permitted limited graduate student

participation.  Once this was effected, the undergraduate
majors, with a little help from their postgraduate friends,
began to organize and repeat the process.  This phenomenon
was so striking and has received so little attention in comparison to the other disturbances and changes universities
have undergone in recent years that a graduate student enrolled
in courses offered by the senior author undertook a follow-
up study.  We will have more to say, particularly from the
student point of view, about this "quiet revolution" later.

Eight of the chairmen decried the "bigness" of the university.  "There are a lot of people out there I don't know
anything about, and it's not all my fault.  This place is too
big," said a chairman in Education.  A chairman in Fine and
Professional Arts complained that the "administration never
fires; they just hire more and try to work around the incompetents."  One of his colleagues in the same college complained
that the tremendous increase in administrative personnel
experienced during the previous five years made his job more
complicated as well as defeating attempts to improve the
student-faculty ratio.  The chairman of a social science
department commented on this large size and complexity by
asserting that even the chairmen--let alone faculty and
students--were ignorant of official channels of communication:
"When the faculty and students don't know about channels they
don't exist--and they therefore don't know how to cope."

The chairmen were extremely critical of the administrative
or non-academic service offices.  Too little of a constructive
nature, for example, was read by them in area newspapers.  At
least ten chairmen could give examples of stories which the

University News Service refused to release because they judg
them to be "not newsworthy."  Some of these same chairmen
placed part of the blame for the Town-Gown cleavage on the
unwillingness of the News Service to emphasize the "good new
of the university.

Again Maintenance was singled out most frequently among
the staff offices for being non-responsive as well as for
levying inconsistent and inflated charges.  One chairman tol
of having maintenance done in his department by a local
business firm at half the price quoted by the Maintenance
office.  The Student Affairs-Academic Affairs bifurcation wa
again deplored:  "We split the student into components,"
said one chairman in the College of Education, "and nobody
looks at the total student."  The perceived goal displacemer
of the non-academic offices was expressed in the following
way by a chairman in the College of Business Administration:
"The Student Affairs office, the Registrar, Special and Publ
Events--all of the people in [Vice President for Administrat
Roskens' shop--exist only to make my life and the student's
life easier.  Why is it so hard to deal with them?"

*References*

1.  T. George Harris, "Warren Bennis, A Conversation," *Psychology Today*,
    3, February 1970, p. 50.

CHAPTER FOUR:  THE FACULTY

Perhaps we should have retitled this chapter The *Faculties*.
It is quite clear from our interviews that faculty members
live and work in academic departments, relatively isolated
from colleagues in other disciplines.  Before considering the
communication problems of the Kent State University faculty,
it might be wise to consider  how they got the way they are.

Although it may come as a shock to their students, professors were once children.  Like other children, their
acquisition of communication skills began, of course, with
listening and speaking.  This is accomplished without the
assistance of the formal educational system.  The reading
and writing skills, however, are acquired only in school by
most children.

As the student progresses through formal education, his
natural preference for oral-aural communication is denied by
the increasing emphasis upon writing-reading skills.  Aptitudes
in the latter determine largely his academic intelligence, or
I.Q., as well as his performance on written ("entrance")
examinations necessary for those who wish to pursue a college
education.  Indeed, he will probably be encouraged to seek a
higher education only if he has demonstrated his proficiency
in writing and reading.

If adept enough at the visual, or linear, communication
skills to find himself enrolled in college he will also find

himself less and less, by comparison with his secondary education, engaging in the oral-aural communication process of
the classroom; rather, he finds himself more and more by
himself, reading books and writing papers outside of class.
If he can distinguish himself by these activities, it is
likely that he will be encouraged to pursue a postgraduate
degree.

The education of the graduate student--from a communica
tion point of view--is a socialization process by which his
appreciation for, and time-spent-in, written communication i
significantly increased at the expense of his oral-aural
communication.  He spends less time in fewer classes than he
did even as an undergraduate; he will read and write even
more.  If the attempt to "socialize" (the word takes on an
ironic meaning in this context) his communication behavior i
successful, he will begin to identify less with his university, which must be held together by oral channels, and more
with the "Invisible College" of his academic discipline whic
is held together by the written channels of discipline-
oriented journals, monographs and books.

The three main hurdles for the graduate student pursuin
the terminal degree--the doctorate--are:  (1) a *written* exam
ination by which he demonstrates his ability to *read* one or
two foreign languages; (2) a *written* examination, called
"comprehensives" or "prelims" or "qualifiers," by which he
demonstrates his knowledge of the field; and (3) a *written*
document, called a dissertation, by which he demonstrates hi
ability to conceive, execute, and write the results of a
research project.  The oral examinations associated with the

second and third hurdles are ritualistic and often meaning-
less.

If the graduate student can clear these reading-writing
hurdles he will be inducted into the "Invisible College" of
his discipline.   Quite likely he will seek a job in some other
college or university.   He will soon learn that to be promoted
it will be necessary to produce a long list of *publications,*
written communications prepared for the journals of his discipline.   The more ambitious he is, the more time he will
allot to research and writing--leaving less time for oral
communication with students, professors in other departments
and administrators.   Thus, the more successful he becomes the
more  oriented he is to the written channels of the discipline.
This, in turn, results in a disintegrating effect upon the
university which can only be held together by oral channels.
The socialization process will be complete when he has the
opportunity to engage in oral communication with his colleagues
in the "Invisible College"--at the annual convention of the
discipline--and finds that the most important function of such
meetings is for the professors to "read papers" to each other.
The "papers" are carefully written linear documents; often
one is not allowed to interrupt the "speaker" and often there
is insufficient time in which to ask questions of the person
who has read the paper.   By this time the socialization process
is complete; the student has moved into a different communication culture, a print or linear culture.   He has become the
"abcedminded" professor, to borrow from the logodelics of
James Joyce.

This analysis has not taken into account the self-selection

process.  Naturally there will be among faculty members a
number of "bookworms" who needed little of the socialization
process described above--at least in regard to reading.  It
is also probably true that a student who elects to attend a
large university rather than a small liberal arts college has
accepted the fact that he will be entering a cold and imper-
sonal experience.  Nonetheless, if our analysis is correct
we should expect to find *a clash of communication cultures*
when the orally-oriented undergraduate is thrown into contact
with his print-oriented professors.

First, however, we should examine how our sample[1] of
Kent State faculty members viewed their communication difficulties *vis a vis* the administration; these problems are
categorized in Table 1.  Only thirty-three faculty members

FACULTY-ADMINISTRATION COMMUNICATION PROBLEMS
(As Seen By Faculty   N=120)

No Problems . . . . . . . . . . . . . . . . . . . . . . 33

Don't Know (Little or No Contact) . . . . . . . . . . . 26

Serious Problems in Communication . . . . . . . . . . . 61

    Too Much Written Communication  . . . . . . . . . . 37
    University Too Large, Complex . . . . . . . . . . . 30
    President White Isolated from Faculty . . . . . . . 25
    Administration Doesn't Listen to Faculty. . . . . . 24
    Unclear About Administrative Duties . . . . . . . . 20
    Faculty Isolated from Administration. . . . . . . . 15
    Administration Uninformed . . . . . . . . . . . . . 15
    Too Much Reliance on Committees . . . . . . . . . . 14
    Long Chain of Command . . . . . . . . . . . . . . . 8
    Goal and Role of University Not Clear . . . . . . . 6

TABLE 1

(less than twenty-eight percent) told us that they felt communication between the two groups either was basically good

or that they perceived no problems.  Nineteen of those thirty-three faculty members were in the College of Education. Twenty-six faculty members (almost twenty-two percent) told us that *they had so little contact with the administration that they did not know whether or not there were communication problems*.  We must interpret this lack of awareness, this lack of contact as a communication problem of sorts in itself.

The answers given by the sixty-one faculty members (over fifty percent) who could *explicitly* identify faculty-administration communication problems are listed in ten categories in Table 1.  The single largest category--"Too Much Written Communication" may seem to contradict our previous analysis about the print-oriented faculty.  In this case, however, the faculty seems to have realized that a *working organization*, as opposed to an international academic discipline, must depend upon oral channels.  In addition, the faculty were complaining that unlike their professional journals which contain debate and a wide variety of points of view, the administration's written vehicles constituted a *one-way medium*.  They felt that they were being buried under an avalanche of written messages: from the President, Provost, deans, chairmen, committees; minutes of the Faculty Senate, Graduate Council, college faculty meetings, department faculty meetings; and, to judge from our interviews, memoranda from practically every administrative office on the campus.

The only way to survive, said one faculty member, is to practice "selective neglect."  But there is the uneasy feeling among many that it may be the crucial document which is neglected.  The most frustrating element of this volume of

paper was expressed by the professor who said, "It is all
downhill." "It's all one-way," our interviewers were told
over and over again. One professor told of writing a length
response to one such document from the Provost's office. Th
response from that office to his memo was--a mimeographed
form letter. This was more than most received; repeatedly w
were told of memoranda and letters written by the faculty to
their administrators which went unanswered and even unacknow
edged. To repeat, the most consistent complaint of the facu
was that their only contact with the administration was to b
on the receiving end of one-way, downward-directed, written
communication. To put this complaint into some perspective,
it should be noted that one dean asserted that the chairmen
and faculty brought part of this paper down on their head by
a distrustful, legalistic, "Put-it-in-writing" attitude; and
the *FYI* and *Official Bulletin* were often exempted from the
complaint.

The second most frequently mentioned problem was the
assertion that communication at KSU was hopeless because of
the awesome size and complexity of the university. A "jungl
"a vast and elaborate bureaucracy," "a complicated cobweb"
are just some of the terms which cropped up in our interview
as faculty members attempted to describe this problem. It i
quite clear that the faculty was overwhelmed by, and ignoran
of, the structure of Kent State University. For example, we
asked the faculty to identify the four main divisions of the
university. We accepted as "correct" any answer which ident
fied either the title of the division or its functions or th
name of the Vice President in charge of the division. Even

with such a liberal grading policy, the faculty failed the
test. Only twenty four (exactly twenty percent) of our
faculty sample gave four "correct" answers.

The four divisions and the faculty's ability to identify
them are listed in Table 2.

FACULTY ABLE TO IDENTIFY MAJOR DIVISIONS OF KSU

| | Yes | No | Total |
|---|---|---|---|
| Academic Affairs (V.P. Harris). . . . . . . | 89 | 31 | 120 |
| Student Affairs (V.P. Matson). . . . . . . . | 74 | 46 | 120 |
| Business and Finance (V.P. Dunn) . . . . . . | 69 | 51 | 120 |
| Administration (V.P. Roskens). . . . . . . . | 66 | 54 | 120 |

TABLE 2

As expected, the faculty were more familiar with the division
of Academic Affairs than with any of the others, but a dis-
tressing twenty-five percent flunked even on that item. The
least known division was Administration, where forty-five percent of the faculty could name neither the name of the division
nor its functions nor its Vice President. And the inverviews
were conducted during a period in which the entire university
was engaging in intense introspection.

The helplessness of the faculty is made clear also by
their lack of knowledge about the "official channels" available to faculty and students. We listed five problems which
a student might face and asked each faculty member to identify
the official channels designated to handle them. The results
are summarized in Table 3. Those who could list each step of
the channels were categorized in the "Yes" column. Those who
did not know the complete procedure but who knew at least the

"First Step" are so categorized.  Those who had no idea of
the channels were listed in the "No" category.  The data spea

FACULTY ABLE TO IDENTIFY OFFICIAL CHANNELS
FOR STUDENT PROBLEMS AT KSU

|  | Yes | First Step | No | Total |
|---|---|---|---|---|
| Unfair Grades. . . . . . . . . . . . . . . | 42 | 47 | 31 | 120 |
| Poor Advising. . . . . . . . . . . . . . | 14 | 62 | 44 | 120 |
| Parking and Traffic. . . . . . . . . . . | 1 | 95 | 24 | 120 |
| Academic Rules and Regulations . . . . . | 12 | 59 | 49 | 120 |
| Social Rules and Regulations . . . . . . | 54 | 2 | 64 | 120 |

TABLE 3

for themselves.  To repeat the statement quoted earlier by a
department chairman, "When the faculty and students don't
know about channels they don't exist--and they therefore don'
know how to cope."  A statement from one of the academic dea
is also appropriate:  "It's time we stopped putting students
down with this 'official channels' talk."

The third most frequent criticism of the faculty was the
by now oft-repeated assertion that President White was isolat
from the faculty.  Twenty-five professors, only *one* of whom
was from the College of Education, expressed this view.  One
Instructor of English felt that the President and his adminis
tration, paraphrasing Rod McKuen, "look through rearview
mirrors," seeing only the faculty and students of the past.
It would be pointless, however, to elaborate further on this
problem.

The fourth most frequent criticism of the faculty was

that the administration did not listen to them. This appears
to be a variant of the "isolation" problem. It was the judgment that the administration would listen only to its own
"party line" being played back to itself by its friends: the
"Cleopatra Syndrome." Only the "good guys," said one professor, get a hearing with the administration. Three professors maintained that their views were so unwelcome that
they had not been able to establish either formal or informal
channels. "There is no open door in the administration," said
another. One professor in Arts and Sciences illustrated this
point by recalling that "eighty of us [faculty members] requested a meeting with the President on May 3, but he turned
us down. We might have been able to help."

The fifth most frequent problem was a variant of the size
and complexity complaint. In connection with that problem we
discussed the startling degree to which the faculty was ignorant of the structure of the university. Twenty of our faculty
subjects volunteered that they did not understand the nature
of administrative duties and responsibilities. "Top heavy,"
and "too many administrators," were phrases they used to make
the point that they had been unable to understand the administration well enough to fix responsibility for past and future
decisions. The consequences of this ignorance were many.
Inability to locate responsibility caused faculty members to
give up pursuing important issues. Many faculty expressed
guilt for sending students out "blind," to be "bounced around
from office to office," particularly in the Business and
Finance, and Student Affairs offices. This widespread ignorance of the system and its accompanying anxiety were so

serious that the faculty interviewees were sometimes briefly
reluctant to cooperate with this study--for fear that it woul
necessarily recommend additional offices and bureaucratizatio

The sixth problem was one of faculty isolation from the
administration and its decision-making process.  This is the
opposite side of the coin in which they pointed out the isolation of the President from the faculty.  The fifteen facult
members who volunteered this problem complained that "we neve
find out. about projects and decisions till they're done," tha
the administration failed to inform the faculty about important decisions and the *whys* of the decisions until it was too
late to consider alternatives.  One example which several
faculty members mentioned to us was a decision to cut down
trees for an expanded parking lot on the front campus.  Practically no one on campus knew of the decision until students
observed construction workers cutting down the trees.  The
campus was extremely tense for a period because of a threaten
"tree-in" until the students and faculty were pacified by
the knowledge that additional trees were being planted to
compensate for the loss.

The seventh problem was simply that even if a faculty
member could get through to an administrator, the latter
either did not know the answer to his question or chose not
to give an answer.

The eighth problem was a frustration with the slowness
of decision-making coupled with the diagnosis that it was
caused by an undue reliance upon committees and commissions.
Part of the professors were upset that the multiplicity of
committees existed as a democratic facade for highly centrali

decision-making, but a tiny minority of them seemed to yearn for genuine autocracy. Again in the interest of balanced perspective, one member of the administration admitted to being baffled by the contradictory demands for "participatory democracy" on one hand, and "strong, decisive leadership" on the other.

That the chain of command from the professor to the ultimate decision center was too long was the ninth problem raised by the faculty. Eight members of our sample mentioned this problem along with the observation that one could "never be sure that the message was relayed--nor that it was relayed as intended." The academic chain-of-command so suffered from "layerism" that many of the faculty, even if they understood the structure of the university, simply assumed that communication was impossible.

The tenth problem, unlike the other nine, focused upon the *content*--or rather its absence--of communication rather than upon the media, channels and practices of communication at KSU. Six members of our faculty sample volunteered that the administration had not spoken clearly on the goals of the university. "There is no vision of where we want to go," one chairman had told us. A faculty member who raised this problem wanted an answer from the administration to the question, "What do we want to do and be good at?"

Before turning to the faculty's relationship with collegial and departmental offices it seems appropriate to consider university sources of information perceived by the faculty to be most and least credible. Table 4 lists the most credible sources as seen by members of the four undergraduate

colleges.  President White was again the single most credible
source, but there is a measure of the professional identifica
tion we mentioned earlier in the collegial percentage of

FACULTY'S MOST CREDIBLE SOURCES

| Source | A&S N=56 | Ed. N=27 | F&PA N=22 | B.A. N=15 | Totals N=120 |
|---|---|---|---|---|---|
| President White | 20 | 18 | 9 | 7 | 54 |
| Presidential Office & Media (*FYI*, etc.) | 11 | 6 | 5 | 0 | 22 |
| Vice President and Provost Harris | 11 | 5 | 1 | 5 | 22 |
| Dean Harkness (A&S) | 16 | 1 | 0 | 0 | 17 |
| Dean Schindler (Ed.) | 0 | 9 | 1 | 0 | 10 |
| Dean Flower (F&PA) | 0 | 0 | 9 | 0 | 9 |
| Unnamed Colleagues | 7 | 0 | 1 | 1 | 9 |
| Faculty Senate | 4 | 3 | 2 | 0 | 9 |
| Faculty Ombudsman | 4 | 0 | 4 | 0 | 8 |
| Dean Mullin (B.A.) | 0 | 0 | 0 | 7 | 7 |
| Dean McGrath (Graduate School) | 6 | 0 | 1 | 0 | 7 |
| Vice President Dunn (Bus. & Finance) | 1 | 2 | 1 | 0 | 4 |
| Assistant to President Beer | 1 | 0 | 1 | 2 | 4 |
| AAUP | 3 | 1 | 0 | 0 | 4 |
| *Daily Kent Stater* | 3 | 0 | 1 | 0 | 4 |
| Associate Provost Hall | 0 | 0 | 0 | 3 | 3 |
| Academic Department Offices | 21 | 12 | 18 | 6 | 57 |
| Miscellaneous Sources | 26 | 16 | 12 | 6 | 60 |

TABLE 4

faculty members who so named him:  Education (sixty-six per
cent), Business Administration (forty-seven percent), Fine
and Professional Arts (forty-one percent), and Arts and
Sciences (thirty-six percent).  There is additional support
for our earlier hypothesis that this high rating was partly
due to "positional" credibility rather than to an "earned"
or "artistic" credibility.  In nominating the President, many
faculty added such comments as, "He's believable but I don't

think he says anything." In addition, the faculty demonstrated a high level of faith in the academic chain-of-authority (Vice President and Provost-Dean-Department Chairman), making it increasingly clear *how unfortunate it was that the President neither spoke to the faculty nor activated its chain of authority during the crises of May 1-4.* Finally, the faculty's lack of trust in non-academic areas is seen by the fact that less than one percent of their votes went to sources outside the academic sector.

That this was more than a lack of trust, i.e., that it may have been an active distrust, can be seen by examining Table 5. Two of the three least credible sources were Vice Presidents Matson and Roskens, each of whom was named only once by the faculty as a most credible source; therefore, their "net" credibility evaluation was decidedly negative. (Remarkedly so with Roskens, who was also the Vice President least known to the faculty.) In addition, thirty-seven of the fifty-seven "Miscellaneous" sources were located in the non-academic divisions.

*The data also suggest that the faculty, by its least credible nominations, had detected an administrative infrastructure.* Although no single interviewee presented an integrated analysis, there was commonality in their reasons for nominating certain individuals and bodies. For example, it was repeatedly pointed out to us that the three least credible individuals--Matson, White and Roskens--were all trained in colleges of Education. Matson and Roskens held academic rank in KSU's College of Education, and upon resigning from the presidency, White revealed that he planned to

FACULTY'S LEAST CREDIBLE SOURCES

| Source | A&S N=56 | ED. N=27 | F&PA N=22 | B.A. N=15 | Totals N=120 |
|---|---|---|---|---|---|
| *Daily Kent Stater* | 8 | 6 | 3 | 4 | 21 |
| Vice President Matson (Student Affairs) | 11 | 2 | 6 | 1 | 20 |
| Student Rumor Mill | 8 | 3 | 4 | 3 | 18 |
| President White & Media (*FYI*, etc.) | 8 | 0 | 5 | 2 | 15 |
| Vice President Roskens (Administration) | 5 | 1 | 4 | 0 | 10 |
| Faculty Rumor Mill | 5 | 3 | 2 | 0 | 10 |
| Dean Harkness (A&S) | 8 | 0 | 1 | 0 | 9 |
| Campus Security & Police | 5 | 3 | 0 | 0 | 8 |
| Faculty Senate | 4 | 1 | 0 | 2 | 7 |
| Upper Administration | 3 | 0 | 2 | 1 | 6 |
| AAUP | 1 | 2 | 0 | 3 | 6 |
| Dean Flower (F&PA) | 0 | 1 | 4 | 0 | 5 |
| Vice President & Provost Harris | 4 | 0 | 0 | 0 | 4 |
| Dean Mullin (B.A.) | 0 | 0 | 0 | 3 | 3 |
| Parking & Traffic Office | 1 | 0 | 1 | 1 | 3 |
| Dean McGrath (Graduate School) | 2 | 0 | 0 | 1 | 3 |
| Library | 1 | 0 | 0 | 1 | 2 |
| Faculty Ombudsman | 2 | 0 | 0 | 0 | 2 |
| Vice President Dunn (Administration) | 2 | 0 | 0 | 0 | 2 |
| President Dix (Board of Trustees) | 0 | 0 | 2 | 0 | 2 |
| Academic Department Offices | 6 | 2 | 2 | 2 | 12 |
| Miscellaneous Sources | 17 | 19 | 13 | 8 | 57 |

TABLE 5

return to teaching in the same college. In addition, we were repeatedly told that the Faculty Senate--whose Chairman enjoyed a close friendship with President White dating back to the days when they were fellow graduate students--was not credible because it and its executive committee were dominated by College of Education professors who were too avidly pro-administration. Finally, when we consider the least credible votes for these four sources--President White, the Faculty Senate and Vice Presidents Matson and Roskens--it is interesti

to note that *over ninety-two percent* of the votes came from
colleges other than Education.  Or, to look at it from another
angle, the faculty of the College of Education cast *less than
one percent* of their least credible votes for those sources,
even though they cast almost *twenty percent* of the total
votes (unlike the other colleges, four Education professors
said that *all* university sources were credible and three more
refused to list least credible sources).  Thus, we see again
the professional identification of the Education faculty
with those sources.  In conclusion, the faculty of the Colleges
of Arts and Sciences, Fine and Professional Arts and Business
Administration seem to have perceived an administration-College
of Education-Faculty Senate infrastructure from which the
Vice Presidents for Business and Finance (Dunn) and Academic
Affairs (Harris) were largely excluded.

Surprisingly few criticisms were raised by the faculty
in regard to communication with their dean and college office.
The few complaints centered around the inaccessibility of a
dean and that faculty inputs were not sought in the collegial
decision-making process.  The complaints seemed to be consistent from college to college.

Intra-departmental communication ranged from "beautiful"
(Sociology) to "too large for effective communication" (English).
Faculty members in several departments complained of a ty-
rannical chairman.  In at least two departments interviewees
reported that a majority had presented their departmental
grievances to the dean--and received no response.  "How does
a majority get rid of a chairman?" asked one professor.

The chief departmental difficulties were with (1) secretive, autocratic chairmen (some departments, surprisingly, operated without even an executive committee as a policy-making body); and (2) an unmanageably large faculty (complicated by the need to schedule all available space for classes, thus eliminating meeting times at which all faculty members could attend); and (3) a lack of physical propinquity (the School of Art, for example, had faculty housed in ten different buildings).

In support of the analysis given at the beginning of this chapter, i.e., that the faculty members have been socialized into a communication culture characterized by departmental insulation and a preoccupation with the print media of the discipline, twenty-six members of our faculty sample volunteered that there was little or no communication among faculty across departmental lines. "Fragmented," "no cross-pollination," "no interplay--either formal or informal," and "so specialized we can't talk to each other," were typical of the remarks. "I feel closer to colleagues in the discipline on either coast than I do to the guy across the hall in another department," said another. "I feel loyalty to the department, not the university," said still another. The consequence of this "communication culture" is the disintegration of the student's education.

It is the faculty-student interface which poses perhaps the greatest communication problem unearthed in this study. "Communication has broken down between the faculty and students," one dean asserted. A majority of the faculty would seem to agree. Many faculty eyes were opened during those days in May when they opened their homes to students and

classes.  "We had an orgy of flexibility and humaneness in
those days," said another dean shortly after that period,
"but already the Counter Reformation has set in--business as
abnormal!"

The facts:   thirty-six members of our faculty sample of
120 volunteered that more contact--both formal and informal--
was needed between faculty and students; thirty-seven faculty
members admitted that the academic advising program had broken
down; eighteen professors said that it was almost impossible
to communicate with students when they were outside the classroom; fifteen professors said that student participation in
decision-making was inadequate; fourteen professors felt that
their classes were too large to permit communication with
students--either in or out of class; twelve professors felt
that the primary emphasis at KSU was on postgraduate education
rather than undergraduate; nine professors said that students
had not tried to initiate communication with professors and
advisors; seven professors said that poor teaching was widespread.

These problems present a depressing picture of the
university--a picture of disintegration.  The oral-aural
systems of communication needed to integrate such a huge
organization were clearly non-existent.  The faculty had
little communication with people outside departmental walls;
hence, it had little knowledge of and loyalty to the larger
organization.  Its preoccupation with the written media of
the various disciplines produced a serious blockage where the
greatest amount of communication should have taken place--
between themselves and their students.  Their ignorance of the

university, other departments and the professors working in
them made professors all but useless--as they freely admitted-
as academic advisors.  "It's in the catalogue," was the best
advice many could give.  Some were not willing to give that
much.

*References*

1.  We were able to interview 120 of the 150 faculty members selected
    by means of a table of random numbers.  The faculty total for
    1969-70 was approximately 1100, giving us a sample of over ten
    percent.  Every academic department of the university was repre-
    sented.

CHAPTER FIVE:   THE STUDENTS

In a recent survey of studies done at the University of
Kansas, Giffin reported that lack of communication--or "Communication Denial"--can be one of the major causes of social
alienation.  Social alienation, he continued, "is not disagreement with another person, even if the disagreement is
severe, so long as interaction continues.  When a person
functionally accepts the conclusion that he cannot communicate with another person or persons--that it is pointless to
try further, social alienation has occurred."[1]  It is the
thesis of this chapter that a large percentage of KSU students
suffered from social alienation by communication denial,
denial from professors, administrators, secretaries and even
from bureaucrats whose ostensible function is to provide
student services.  The denial can be subtle, even non-verbal;
simple discourtesy can produce the effect.  A lack of understanding of the university, such as where to turn for help,
can also produce withdrawal and alienation.

Students at KSU did not understand even the basics of
the structure of the university.  When asked to name the four
divisions--either by title or by function or by the name of
each Vice President--only *two* of 225 student subjects could
correctly identify all four.  Only fifty-five of the 225
could name even *one* of the four divisions.  One undergraduate
student in Business Administration responded to the question

by saying: "I have no idea--they [Vice Presidents] must wear masks and drive at night. Secretive men." Another student responded by saying: "I don't know. If I thought it would do any good I might try to get to know them."

STUDENTS ABLE TO IDENTIFY OFFICIAL CHANNELS
FOR STUDENT PROBLEMS AT KSU

|  | Yes | First Step | No | Total |
|---|---|---|---|---|
| Unfair Grades | 2 | 97 | 126 | 225 |
| Poor Advising | 0 | 134 | 91 | 225 |
| Parking and Traffic | 0 | 150 | 75 | 225 |
| Academic Rules and Regulations | 2 | 78 | 145 | 225 |
| Social Rules and Regulations | 26 | 59 | 140 | 225 |

TABLE 1

Table 1 presents student responses to questions about official channels for handling five kinds of student problems. The "Yes" column includes the students who could explain all of the steps involved, the "First Step" column indicates the number of students who knew where to begin in an attempt to solve their problems and the "No" category indicates the students who did not know even the first step. For example, a student in Business Administration told one of our interviewers: "I have a grade problem now and I wish I knew where to go." Knowing the first step is not enough if that person has a vested interest to be protected by not sending him to the second step. Again we feel the data speak for themselves.

We should not assume that even if the official channels were known to the students that they would work satisfactorily

Students told us, for example, of having complained about
poor academic advising to their departmental and collegial
offices, but that it "got nowhere," as one put it.   In addition,
department chairmen told us quite openly that it was difficult,
if not impossible, to reverse a professor on such problems.
The "use the channels" argument seems to be specious, a method
for putting off students.   In short, the overwhelming majority
of Kent State University students understood neither the basic
structure of the university nor the official channels established to deal with their problems.   Many who did understand
them had found them to be of little help.

Our first question on internal communication to the 225
students was a request for them to identify problems they
had experienced during their career at Kent.   The answers to
this non-directive, open-ended question are presented in
Table 2.   Over sixty-seven percent of the students listed at

STUDENTS' COMMUNICATION PROBLEMS

No Problems. . . . . . . . . . . . . . . . . . . . . . . . . 74

Serious Problems . . . . . . . . . . . . . . . . . . . . . .151

    Confusion of Responsibility ("Run Around"). . . . . . . 63
    Service Offices Unresponsive. . . . . . . . . . . . . . 35
    Academic Advising . . . . . . . . . . . . . . . . . . . 23
    Faculty Inaccessible. . . . . . . . . . . . . . . . . . 18
    University Too Large, Too Complex . . . . . . . . . . . 14
    Bureaucratic Slowness . . . . . . . . . . . . . . . . . 12
    Administration Isolated from Students . . . . . . . . .  5
    Secretaries ("Gatekeepers") . . . . . . . . . . . . . .  4
    Miscellaneous Problems. . . . . . . . . . . . . . . . . 17

TABLE 2

least one problem; the most frequently mentioned problem was
what we have called confusion of responsibility or--the "run

around." By this the students meant that they were unable
to find sources who could help them solve their problem, indeed that no one even knew where to send them for such help.
"Generally people do not want to be bothered; they just push
you off to someone else--one sends you to another," was one
student remark typical of this category. Accompanying this
confusion of responsibility was the students' perception of
hostility expressed toward them when seeking information,
and which constituted a form of communication denial.

The second problem--service offices unresponsive--is a
variation of the first problem, but with specificity in
locating where they had met such denial. "The Student Teaching Office is just discourteous," was a typical remark. The
Housing Office, Records Office, Registrar's Office, Student
Activities Office, Parking and Traffic Office were all cited
for their lack of helpfulness, if not open hostility toward
students.

The third problem, academic advising was one of the most
scandalous problems we discovered. "It's hard to get one,"
"It's hard to find out who they are," "Difficult to make
appointments with them," and "You wait a long time to see
them," were all typical complaints. We followed up this
problem by a specific direct question about academic advising.
In Table 3 we find that fifty-two percent of our student
sample said that they either had never talked to their advisor
(including a large group who were not aware of having one) or
said that they had experienced problems in trying to communicate with their advisor. The latter group made such comments
as:

A. "They don't do a damned thing so I depend on friends and sorority sisters."

B. "My advisor is not useful. He doesn't seem interested in helping students. It's hard to see him and he's in a big hurry all the time."

STUDENT-ADVISOR COMMUNICATION

| | No Problems | No Contact | Problems | Totals |
|---|---|---|---|---|
| Arts & Sciences | 40 | 18 | 22 | 80 |
| Education | 30 | 11 | 22 | 63 |
| Fine & Professional Arts | 25 | 10 | 14 | 49 |
| Business Administration | 13 | 14 | 6 | 33 |
| TOTALS | 108 | 53 | 64 | 225 |

TABLE 3

C. "He's usually not in. When he's in he's too busy to talk. He treats you as one of many, not as an individual with individual problems."

D. "I went to see him once and he humiliated me; he said if I had to ask a question like that--it was about scheduling--I shouldn't be in the university. I haven't been back."

E. "He's no help whatsoever. He's old, incompetent, uninterested and doesn't know the answers."

F. "I couldn't see one for three years. The secretary told me to read the catalogue."

G. "They don't know anything about the courses and instructors outside the department."

H.  "She's never in her office."

I.  "He acts as if it bothers him to talk to me."

J.  "I tried once and had to wait for over an hour.
    And it was so impersonal."

K.  "It takes three weeks to get an appointment with
    her.  She's always gone to conventions and meetings."

L.  "[a co-ed] He says he's my personal advisor, not my
    academic advisor."

M.  "I couldn't understand the catalogue so I went to
    see him.  He told me to read it again."

This last bit of advice may have come from one of those
faculty members who objected so loudly to one-way, downward-
directed, *written* communication.  It is significant that many
students found that their professors "don't know anything
about the courses and instructors outside the department."
These comments, plus sarcastic remarks about "scholars" who
are isolated except for their books indicate an intuitive
understanding of the clash of communication cultures between
faculty and students.

Closely related to the advising problem was the fourth
category--the inaccessibility of the faculty.  The chief
problem was in finding professors outside of class, that
office hours--even when kept--were established strictly for
the convenience of the faculty, not students.  This was
especially true for commuting and working students.

The fifth problem volunteered by the students was the
large size of the university, college, department and classes.
It is quite clear that the students understood that they could
not approach a professor when there were hundreds of students

in a class.  It appears to be a kind of contractual communication self-denial.

These last two problems were further supported by student response to a direct follow up question concerning student-instructor communication.  Fifty nine or twenty-six percent reported having experienced difficulties in communicating with their instructors either because they could not meet with them outside of the classroom or because they felt that the large size of classes precluded any personal attention from the instructors.

The sixth problem was the complaint about bureaucratic slowness, that solving even a simple problem seemed to involve so many offices and so much time that students lost interest in its resolution.  The seventh problem, volunteered by four students, was that secretaries were nasty to them, particularly when playing the role of "Gatekeeper," i.e., in keeping students away from their boss.  The miscellaneous problems were too diffuse to summarize.

We also asked direct questions about student communication with their college and departmental offices.  Sixteen percent of the 225 students reported having difficulties with both offices (only seventy-two percent reported direct contact with their college office while eighty-seven percent reported such contact with the department of their major).

Because of our interest in the "quiet revolution" at KSU, the drive on the part of students to organize and press for participation in departmental decision-making, Jane Haenle conducted a follow-up study of this phenomenon by means of in-depth interviews with twenty of the university's

twenty-four representatives to the Graduate Student Council.
Each one represented students in the different departments
offering graduate programs.  Thus, Mrs. Haenle's study offers
a department by department picture of student penetration into
decision making.  The twenty representatives were not "kids,"
but mature adults with a mean age of 28.2 years; they were
emphatic, partly because of their teaching responsibilities,
about wanting to join the "community of scholars" in the
department.

The representatives characterized their departmental
associations of graduate students in the following ways:   ten
reported "strong" or "fairly strong" associations; six reported that the students were just beginning to organize;
three reported no association and no plans to organize one;
the remaining representative characterized his department's
graduate student association as "weak."  Not surprisingly,
Haenle found that the six departments where students were
just beginning to organize were also the six departments
where students were not involved in committees and departmental
decision-making.  Three of the representatives reported departmental hostility toward their attempts to organize (open
warfare in one department made the representative unwilling
to participate in the study).  Sixteen departments had permitted graduate student participation in governance, eight
of them having alloted votes to students.  Three departments
permitted graduate student votes on the executive committee;
interestingly enough, these three were departments without
associations.  Sixteen departments permitted student membership on graduate-studies committees, thirteen of which had

extended votes to the students.  Practically all of this
penetration had occurred within the previous two years.  Two
of the three departments who were hostile toward the graduate
student association were cases where the students had not
been included in departmental governance.  Consequently,
three of the representatives felt that the role and status
of graduate students could be improved *only by the formation
of a labor union*.  A fourth representative said that he had
begun to consider this possibility.  Thus, it would appear
that an intransigence on the part of a small minority of
departments could bring about the formation of a labor union
to represent students in all departments.[1]

Such associations were probably beginning to emerge
because students--both postgraduate and undergraduate--
lacked faith in the ability of student government to deal with
their real problems.  When asked about their dealings with
student government, 167 of the 225 students said that they
had had little or no contact with it.  "No, practically
unaware of it.  I don't know who they are and don't care.
They don't do anything for me," said a student in Arts and
Sciences.  A student in Education said:  "It's a farce.
There's no reason to have it.  No power.  Only declarations."
"I was a member," said a Geography major, "and it's a chaotic
organization.  It should have improved communication; it would
take a year of comprehensive study to change it, but it could
be a valuable link between students, faculty and administration."  Additional evidence for this assessment can be seen
by comparing the most and least credibility ratings for student government.  In Table 4, the most credible sources,

STUDENTS' MOST CREDIBLE SOURCES

Faculty (General and Specific). . . . . . . . . . . . . . 124
President White (and Presidential Media). . . . . . . . . . 94
*Daily Kent Stater* . . . . . . . . . . . . . . . . . . . . 43
Department Chairmen and Offices . . . . . . . . . . . . . . 31
Dormitory Staff and Media . . . . . . . . . . . . . . . . . 30
WKSU (Campus Radio Station) . . . . . . . . . . . . . . . . 27
Roommate. . . . . . . . . . . . . . . . . . . . . . . . . . 24
Administration in General . . . . . . . . . . . . . . . . . 18
Student Government. . . . . . . . . . . . . . . . . . . . . 15
Student Affairs Offices . . . . . . . . . . . . . . . . . . 10
No One. . . . . . . . . . . . . . . . . . . . . . . . . . . 7
Vice President Matson (Student Affairs) . . . . . . . . . . 6
Vice President Harris (Academic Affairs). . . . . . . . . . 5
Records Office. . . . . . . . . . . . . . . . . . . . . . . 5
No Answer . . . . . . . . . . . . . . . . . . . . . . . . . 4
Information Center. . . . . . . . . . . . . . . . . . . . . 4
Newsrap . . . . . . . . . . . . . . . . . . . . . . . . . . 3
Miscellaneous Sources . . . . . . . . . . . . . . . . . . . 40

TABLE 4

student government was named by fifteen students; in Table 5, the least credible sources, it was named by twenty-one student giving it a net credibility rating on the negative side. The vast majority, however, did not consider it as a source of information at all.

The more significant conclusion about the students' most credible sources is the sad fact that *the top four were silent during the crises of May.*

It can be seen by examining Table 5, least credible sources, that each of the four most credible sources, the silent sources, had a net rating which was positive. The conservative nature of Kent State students is suggested by the lack of credibility of groups such as SDS, BUS and YSA (Young Socialists Alliance). Also, having lived through a crisis publicized to the entire world, the students thought of the external mass media--primarily television--as an internal source of information!  And as a source they found

it lacking.

STUDENTS' LEAST CREDIBLE SOURCES

```
Student Rumor Mill. . . . . . . . . . . . . . . . . .50
Faculty Members (General and Specific). . . . . . . . .38
Radical Groups (SDS, BUS, etc.) . . . . . . . . . . . .33
External Mass Media . . . . . . . . . . . . . . . . . .29
Unspecified Word-of-Mouth . . . . . . . . . . . . . . .28
WKSU (Campus Radio Station) . . . . . . . . . . . . . .23
Student Affairs Offices . . . . . . . . . . . . . . . .21
Student Government. . . . . . . . . . . . . . . . . . .21
Daily Kent Stater . . . . . . . . . . . . . . . . . . .21
Administration in General . . . . . . . . . . . . . . .20
No Answer . . . . . . . . . . . . . . . . . . . . . . .20
Department Chairmen and Offices . . . . . . . . . . . .17
No One. . . . . . . . . . . . . . . . . . . . . . . . .14
Campus Security . . . . . . . . . . . . . . . . . . . .11
President White . . . . . . . . . . . . . . . . . . . .10
College Deans and Offices . . . . . . . . . . . . . . .10
Business Offices. . . . . . . . . . . . . . . . . . . . 8
Vice President Matson . . . . . . . . . . . . . . . . . 7
Secretaries . . . . . . . . . . . . . . . . . . . . . . 5
Miscellaneous Sources . . . . . . . . . . . . . . . . .21
```

TABLE 5

To summarize, we found that the students were largely

uninformed about the structure of the university and its

official channels.  We found considerable evidence of social

alienation by communication denial--communication denial at

almost every level and sector of the university.  Academic

advising was found to be outrageously ineffective; student-

faculty communication was basically effective inside the

classroom, but ineffective even there in some of the larger

classes.  The alienation and impersonality seem to be partly

a function of class size, partly a function of the clash of

communication cultures--the linear, print-oriented faculty

which sought to avoid face-to-face communication with students

outside of class--and the orally-oriented students who felt
they were dealt with as numbers, as cattle, if at all.  A
faculty interviewee told us of a sign posted in the English
department after the May tragedy by frustrated students:  "We
publish while you perish."  It was literally true at KSU.

*References*

1.  Jane Haenle, "The Status of the Kent State University Graduate
    Student, 1970-71," unpublished paper prepared for Speech 651,
    Industrial and Organizational Communication.

## CHAPTER SIX:  THE NON-ACADEMIC DIVISIONS

The allegiances of the authors of this book to the academic sector are unavoidable.  We are academicians.  Our
basic assumption in analyzing Kent State University was that
it exists solely to facilitate communication (teaching-
learning) between faculty and students.  The three other
divisions (Student Affairs, Business and Finance, Administration) were seen as support or maintenance services for the
main business of the university--teaching and learning.  How
well did these divisions perform these services?

We shall devote more attention to the Student Affairs
Division than to the  other two.[1]  The sample in this
division included twenty-six of the thirty-nine full-time
staff members in the Student Affairs Division.  The problems
of the university were the problems of the division; the data
suggest that the overall administration of an organization
will determine the administration of a staff office.  This
should be no surprise when one considers that classical
organizational theory (Weber, Urwick, etc.) regards staff
offices as *extensions of the boss*.  Thus, to represent that
boss would be to imitate him--particularly in what we have
already determined to be a highly centralized administration.

For example, the most frequently mentioned problem in
the division supported LaForme's conclusion that the "Vice
President of Student Affairs was not available to a large

portion of the staff." In general, LaForme found that subordinates found it difficult to get feedback from superiors.
In fact, several staff members verbalized a profound distrust
of their superiors in the Student Affairs hierarchy. Although
the division espoused a concept of "functional interdependence" among the various offices in Student Affairs, the
perceptions of horizontal communication by the staff did not
support it as an actuality.

The bifurcation of student affairs and academic affairs,
first mentioned by academic officers, was confirmed by the
most and least credible source nominations within the division.
The faculty, as will be recalled, tended to select from its
own sector its most credible sources and to select its least
credible sources from the non-academic divisions. The Student
Affairs division, however, tended to select both categories
from the non-academic sectors. From a total of ninety-six
votes cast for most and least credible sources, only *twelve
votes* (or twelve percent) went for academic sources (e.g.,
the Faculty Senate and Vice President Harris received votes
as most credible, while the deans of Education and Arts and
Sciences received votes as least credible sources). In other
words, Student Affairs would seem not to be anti-academic,
simply non-academic.

More important, however, is the nature of the interface
between the division and its internal "customers," i.e., the
students. LaForme found that one of the students' most
serious complaints--"the run around"--was confirmed by those
who were accused of the practice. Eight staff members
(almost one-third of the  sample) admitted that students were

submitted to "wild goose chases" and the "run around."  Another large group of staff members expressed doubt that they had established systems by which to know student problems and desires.

This point was clearly supported by student responses to a direct question about their contact with Student Affairs offices.  Of the sample of 225 students, 168 (or *seventy-five percent*) said that they had *had no contact* with the Student Affairs division.  This compares with eighty-five (or thirty-three percent) students who similarly responded to the same question about Business and Finance offices.  Whether or not Student Affairs services were reaching a sufficiently high percentage of students would seem to be a question to be answered by the Student Affairs staff and the students, but it does seem quite clear that if they were in communication with only twenty-five percent of the students, then they were not likely to have a clear picture of student problems and desires.  The picture was even more distorted because that twenty-five percent tended to be those perceived as the "good guys."

As mentioned above, over sixty-six percent of the students reported having contact with the Business and Finance offices.  Only twenty-nine (or thirteen percent) reported having difficulties with them.  Misinformation and a lack of courtesy seem to be the most common complaint.  In addition, students felt that they were not trusted by the various business offices.

Of the three non-academic divisions, it was only in Business and Finance that we did not hear the complaint that

the Vice President (Dunn) was unavailable.  We also found that
the staff members in the business offices--as was the case in
Student Affairs and Administration also--had an almost perfect
understanding of the structure of the university, as would be
expected of staff personnel.  Therefore, it was highly significant when we were repeatedly told by interviewees in the
business offices about the *desperate* need for delegation,
decentralization and trust from President White.

Again, the  most and least credible sources listed by
interviewees in Business and Finance indicated a wall between
themselves and the academic sector.  Only four of fifty-three
such sources named were in the academic sector.

The most vocally anti-academic sector of the university
was the division called Administration.  It is perhaps a
misnomer when one considers that the functions included in
that division are community relations, alumni relations, the
news service and internal communication.  As our data showed
earlier, it was the division and had the Vice President least
known to the faculty and students.  The anti-academic bias
seemed to originate from:   (1) a feeling that the faculty had
received higher salary increases than they had for the past
five to eight years; (2) a feeling that faculty should teach
and not worry about administrative decision-making; and (3)
problems encountered in trying to present the university,
including an "eccentric faculty," in the "best possible
light" to the community, the alumni and public at large.  The
interviewees in the Administrative division said that they
detected a lack of trust of themselves on the part of the
faculty.  This perception was supported by the least credible

ratings given by chairmen and faculty to Vice President Roskens. It was in this division also that *secrecy* emerged as a significant problem. Finally, Vice President Roskens was faulted more by his staff for a lack of accessibility than were the other Vice Presidents--mainly because of frequent trips out of town which made him unavailable for communication.

In short, the non-academic staff offices seemed to echo many of the problems of the university as a whole. In addition, there seemed to be a barrier between them and the academic sector. Both groups had a propensity to talk only with people similar to themselves.

*References*

1. We are deeply indebted to the work of Judie LaForme, member of the Task Force on Communication and participant-observer as a member of the Student Affairs Staff, who conducted most of the interviews in the Student Affairs Division. Her analysis of the data will be submitted for publication elsewhere under the title, "Kent State University Communication Study: Student Affairs Division."

CHAPTER SEVEN:   CONCLUSIONS

It seems conclusive to us that the disintegration of
Kent State University during the crises of May, 1970, can be
traced to certain organization-communication *imperatives*
which were present in the routine functioning of the university:   a highly centralized and indecisive administration
which operated "blind" because of inadequate upward-directed
communication; a President with little appreciation for his
communication responsibilities; the absence of a two-way
system of communication designed to integrate all segments
of the rapidly expanded university; academic officers who
were shut out of administrative decision-making; a fragmented,
print-oriented faculty whose loyalty was to the department
and discipline rather than to the university; large numbers
of students who had been alienated from the university because of communication denial; and non-academic divisions
which were found to be isolated from the academic sector.

During the crisis, the absence of the President and the
absence of clear-cut delegation made it difficult for insiders
and outsiders to cope with the university.  A mistaken
"impression" formed by a university attorney forced the final,
fatal confrontation between the students and Guardsmen.
Nonetheless, the university was less than ineffective in
communicating *vital* information to the university community.

In a close examination of administrative communication

during routine functioning, we found that President White had
failed in his first function as an executive: *to develop
and maintain a system of communication*. His inability to
delegate authority to his Vice Presidents let the latter to
refer to themselves as "assistants to the President." The
academic officers, the deans, were almost unanimous in the
judgment that they had been blocked from providing "academic
input" into the central administrative decision-making
process. The majority of department chairmen repeated this
charge.

Chairmen, faculty and students agreed that the academic
advising program had broken down. Chairmen felt powerless
to deal with incompetent and tenured professors. Professors,
on the other hand, were found to have little loyalty to the
university, being bound to the "Invisible College" of their
discipline by means of books and journals. We found them also
to be ignorant of the structure and channels of the university.

Similarly, students were ignorant of the structure and
channels of the university. Those few students who had
knowledge enough to test the "channels" found them to be
imperfect at best. Academic advising had deteriorated into
a scandalous problem.

A "quiet revolution" was observed at the departmental
level, a revolution in which graduate students were organizing for penetration into departmental decision-making.
Explosive situations were observed in which the final resolution may be the formation of student labor unions.

The four most credible sources of information to students

were also sources which remained silent during the crisis. We also found considerable evidence that students suffered from social alienation by communication denial--communication denial at almost every level and sector of the university.

The non-academic staff offices seemed to echo many of the problems of the university as a whole. In addition, there seemed to be a barrier between the personnel of these divisions and the personnel of the academic sector. Both groups had a propensity to talk only with people similar to themselves.

We have talked much about problems, little about solutions. As Chairman of the university's Task Force on Communication, the senior author proposed many recommendations to the University Commission To Implement a Commitment to Non-Violence. We have included these in Appendix C, and will not discuss them in detail in this chapter. The thrusts of the recommendations, however, should be emphasized. They are: (1) decentralization of authority; (2) personalization of communication; (3) development of two-way channels; and (4) a "flattening" of the pyramid.

It is clear to us (particularly because of a comparative study underway at another Midwestern university) that Kent State cannot long endure in its present centralized condition. Authority must be diffused all the way to the departmental level where needed personalization must take place.

Personalization will occur only when departments begin to innovate. One innovation that we feel to be crucial is that rewards and punishments must be given to the faculty, after consultation with students, on the basis of teaching and advising performance.

We also feel that two-way channels must be developed by which to integrate the university. It will require energy and courage on the part of administration and faculty to do so, but the alternatives are disintegration and alienation.

Finally, a "flattening" of the pyramid known as Kent State University must be effected. A student taking Fundamentals of Speech, for example, is responsible to the Instructor (usually a graduate student) who is responsible to the course coordinator who is responsible to the division chairman who is responsible to the school director who is responsible to the college dean who is responsible to the Vice President and Provost who is responsible to the President who is. . . . This does not mention the secretaries and "assistants-to" and other gatekeepers along the way. The problems of blocked channels and invisible authorities would be alleviated considerably if these status levels could eithe be compressed or reduced.

Finally, we must return to the theme that communication is made increasingly difficult as organizations increase dramatically in size. If we cannot find innovations by which to deal with such large numbers, we will have to face the possibility of retarding growth--perhaps we will even have to face the prospect of dismantling these gigantic institutio The remaining possibility is that they may be dismantled for us, dismantled for us in ways that all reasonable people will despise.

# APPENDICES

APPENDIX A:  METHODOLOGY

The very popular cliche, "Communication breakdown," was the often heard judgment about the May tragedies at Kent State.  At the first faculty meeting of the Division of Rhetoric and Communication following the tragedies a proposal was passed requesting the senior author to conduct an organizational [communication] study of the university to isolate the communication problems causing or adding to the crisis, and recommend solutions.  Immediately, the senior author began to conduct interviews in the manner he had developed during his two summers as a Faculty Research Consultant to NASA's Marshall Space Flight Center in Huntsville, Alabama. He began at the top of the organization and fanned down and out in listening to the administration describe what had happened, what problems they had experienced both in terms of the crisis period as well as during the routine operation of the university.

On May 21, 1970, President Robert I. White established a University Commission to Implement a Commitment to Non-Violence.  The senior author was appointed to the Commission and designated as the Chairman of its Task Force on Communication.  The task force recommended that his study be further expanded to provide additional data for their recommendations. As a result, faculty members, graduate students and under-graduate students of the Division of Rhetoric and Communication as well as members of the task force worked together to construct the standardized interview guide.  The guide was revised six times on the basis of pilot interviews with faculty and students.  In its final form, the questionnaire was divided into four major divisions; [see interview in Appendix B] crisis communication, internal communication on a routine day to day basis, credibility of internal sources of communication, and finally [knowledge of] established channels of communication for solving routine problems.

Within the crisis section, subjects were asked for their major sources of information concerning the events of the first week in May and when and how they first learned about these events.  Specific questions were also asked concerning their knowledge of conditions surrounding the crisis period-- such as "Did you know that assembly [peaceful or otherwise] had been prohibited?"  If the subject answered yes, then follow-up questions were asked to determine when and how they learned of the condition.

Questions on routine internal communication were different for faculty and staff as compared to the student subjects. Faculty members were asked only open-ended questions about their internal communication upward, horizontal, and downward within the organizational structure and solutions they would like to recommend.  Students were first asked an open-ended question about their communication problems within the university.  This question was followed by a series of specific questions on potential problem areas determined during the pilot interviews.

In the third section, all subjects were asked to give the three most credible and three least credible internal sources of information.

In the last section subjects were asked to list the
official channels of communication for solving specific
problems as well as the main divisions of the university and
the Vice Presidents which headed these divisions.

At the time the questionnaire was being developed, the
sample of subjects were also being selected. At the top of
the organizational structure, basically the entire population
was interviewed. In this way, the President, his Executive
Assistant, the four Vice Presidents, all the deans, and twenty-
nine department chairmen were interviewed. The few remaining
chairmen were not interviewed because we were unable to arrange
interviews with them during the summer. Key officials and
staff in the three non-academic sectors, i.e. Student Affairs,
Business and Finance, and Administration, were also interviewed. Because of the size of the faculty and student
populations, it was necessary to draw a sample of each.

To determine the faculty sample, it was necessary to
contact the Deans of each of the four major colleges for
faculty within each college. Each faculty member was then
assigned a number. Using a table of random numbers, a faculty
sample of 150 was selected. After examining the list, we
found that three small departments were not represented within the sample. Therefore, continuing to use the same table
of random numbers, the first faculty member which came up
from each of these departments were added making the final
sample 153. A letter was sent to each faculty member thus
selected explaining the study. Assigned interviewers attempte
to contact each faculty member to arrange an interview.
Interviews were completed for 120 of the sample. These

faculty interviews ran from forty minutes to two and one
half hours.  An interview ran an average of approximately
one and one half hours.  Within the faculty sample, eight
percent were instructors, thirty-nine percent were assistant
professors, twenty-one percent were associate professors, and
thirty-two percent were professors.  They had taught at KSU
from one to thirty-two years.  The mean number of years they
had taught at KSU was 7.7 years; the mode, three years.

By far the most difficult sample to determine was the
student sample.  We were unable to locate any complete, up
to date list of students attending KSU.  Because of the many
problems involved in finishing the term by correspondence
with students spread out over the country, the computers
were all tied up.  As a last resort, we used the student
directory as our base, fully aware that not all students were
listed in it.  From this list, every Nth student was selected,
making a sample of 300.  One of the members of the Task
Force on Communication who had access to a list of current
students checked each one of these names to determine if they
were registered at KSU for spring quarter 1970.  If the subject was no longer at KSU, the next name in the student
directory was selected.  All addresses were updated whenever
possible.  Postcards were sent to all students selected in
the sample briefly explaining the study and requesting that
the students notify us of any time they would be in Kent
willing to be interviewed.  All student subjects were also
cross checked with the list of summer school students, so
that whenever possible we could locate the students in Kent.
Because we preferred a face-to-face interview, if subjects

lived near Kent or if a group of subjects lived in one general area, interviewers arranged series of interviews and drove to those areas. Interviewers living in Cleveland, Akron, Canton and other cities of Northern Ohio interviewed many students at home. When all else failed, interviews were conducted by telephone. Thus, we were finally able to interview 225 students. Some students refused to be interviewed, a few gave reasons which included fears that we either represented the FBI or would turn our findings--including the names of subjects--over to various law enforcement agencies. In some cases, parents refused to let their children talk to us. The saddest reasons, however, for failing to complete interviews were given by parents whose daughter had been hospitalized for a breakdown, or by those parents who had not seen their son for weeks, and who had no idea of his whereabouts. We felt fortunate to have found as many as we did. Of the 225 students finally interviewed, twenty percent were freshmen, nineteen percent were sophomores, fifteen percent were juniors twenty-five percent were seniors , and twenty-one percent were graduate students. These students had attended Kent from one to ten years; thirty-nine percent for one year, twenty-one percent for two years, sixteen percent for three years, thirteen percent for four years, and elevent percent for five or more years. They ranged in age from seventeen to fifty-two, with the mean being twenty-two years and the mode nineteen years of age.

To obtain a more complete overview of what happened at Kent, especially that first week in May, it was also necessary to interview several members of the city and county administration. In addition we used a snowball technique; i.e. when it became apparent that crucial sources of information were named by subjects, they were also contacted and interviewed.

As is obvious from the above explanation, a considerable problem involved obtaining and training enough competent interviewers. Students and faculty of the Division of Rhetoric and Communication and some members of the Task Force on Communication served as interviewers. The interviews of the President, Vice Presidents, Deans, Chairmen, some faculty, students and staff personnel, and the city and county officials were done by the authors. The remaining faculty interviews were conducted by faculty and graduate students within the Division of Rhetoric and Communication. Staff interviews were done by graduate students and Judie LaForme, a member of the Task Force on Communication. Student interviews were completed by students within the Division of Rhetoric and Communication.

Interviewers were directed to read the questions exactly as given on the interview guide. If it was necessary to state the question another way to make it clear to the subject, or to probe a subject for a better understanding of the answer, the interviewer was to indicate that on the guide. The interviewers were instructed to tell no one, even other interviewers, who they were contacting or anything that had been said in interviews. (Only three people, the authors and the secretary of the Division of Rhetoric and Communication, Vicki Byers, know the entire sample.) Many of the interviewers were already well experienced in the necessary techniques as they had just completed an organizational study of a local bank for a graduate course in Organizational Communication taught by the senior author. The other interviewers were trained by observing pilot interviews and evaluating them afterward. As the interviewers were beginning, the senior author frequently called interviewees to request an evaluation of the effectiveness of the interview and interviewer. Some of the interviewers worked on this task as partial fulfillment for college credit. We are greatly indebted to a university grant which allowed us to pay some interviewers for their services and to cover the costs of the telephone calls.

APPENDIX B:   THE INTERVIEW GUIDE

KSU COMMUNICATION PROJECT

Standard Interview Guide

Directions to the Interviewer:

1.  During the approach, emphasize that the interviewee's answers are confidential.  This is *crucial!!!!*

2.  Read the questions as written, *word-for-word*.  Change the wording only when the interviewee does not understand the original wording.  Even then, go back to repeat the original wording.

3.  Probe *only* when the interviewee gives an indication that there is more to the answer than was given.  If you do probe, put an upper case "P" with the answer to it.

4.  Whenever the interviewee mentions the mass media, press him for radio call leters, channel numbers, names of papers and magazines.

5.  Do not *evaluate* any of his answers (either with words or expressions).

6.  Remember that someone else will have to read your answers. Go back over them immediately after the interview and fill in legibly what you were unable to write down accurately at the time.

7.  If you have doubts about how accurately you are getting down his answer, play it back to him in his *own* words and get his reaction.

8.  The information included in [brackets] is for  the benefit of you, the interviewer, and is not to be read aloud to the interviewee.  Information included in (parentheses) is to be read aloud to the interviewee.

9.  In closing, alert the interviewee to the possibility that the Director of the project may telephone him to determine whether or not the interviewee was satisfied with the interview.

10.  Do *not* mention the interviewee's name to anyone, even other interviewers.

I.   Suggested Approach

As you may know, this study is being conducted by the
Task Force on Communication which will report to
President White's Commission to Implement a Commitment
to Non-Violence (Kegley Commission).  From there, the
report will go the President White.

The goals are to identify problems in communication and
make recommendations to improve them--even if changes
in the basic structure of the university are called for.
Therefore, the frankness of your answers is crucial;
you were selected at random and your answers will be
regarded as *strictly confidential*.  Only group findings
will be reported; your name will not even appear in
the report.

There are a number of topics to be covered such as:
communication during crisis, problems in the routine,
day-to-day operation of the university and internal
credibility.  First, however, there is some personal
information we need in order to categorize responses.

II.  Personal Data

A.  Name

B.  [For students]

1.  Student number

2.  Year in college (1st, 2nd, etc.)
    (as of May, 1970)

3.  How long at KSU?

4.  Age at last birthday

5.  Sex [if not obvious]

6.  Where staying (May 1-4)

7.  Race (Do you mind telling me your race?)

8.  College

9.  Major department

10.  Assigned advisor

11.  Do you hold any other position in the university
     beside that of student?

C.  [For others]

1.  Position or title

2.  Immediate supervisor or superior

3.  How long with KSU?

III.  Crisis Communication [If mass media are mentioned, press for radio call letters, channel numbers, names of newspapers and magazines.]

A.  What was the major source of your information about the Friday night (May 1) disturbances in Kent?

(When and how did you *first* hear about it?)

B.  What was the major source of your information about the  Saturday night (May 2) disturbances?

(When and  how did you *first* hear about it?)

C.  What was the major source of your information about the Sunday night (May 3) disturbances?

(When and how did you *first* hear about it?)

D.  What was the major source of your information about the Monday night (May 4) disturbances?

(When and how did you *first* hear about it?)

E.  Since you first heard about these events, what have been your major sources concerning them?

F.  Did you find significant discrepancies between what you first heard and what you have learned since then?

Yes _____   No _____

G.  If yes, what are the discrepancies?  [be sure to record conflicting sources]

H.  Were you aware that a demonstration was scheduled for 12 o'clock on Monday?

Yes _____   No ____

I.  If yes, how were you informed?

J.  Were you aware that curfews were established?

Yes _____   No ____

K.  When and how did you learn that curfews had been established?

L.  Did you know that assembly (peaceful or otherwise)
    had been prohibited?

    Yes _____   No _____

M.  When and how did you learn that assembly had been
    prohibited?

N.  When and how did you learn of the ordered evacuation
    of the campus?

O.  At the time of the Monday rally, who did you think
    had official control of the university?

P.  Did you think that the National Guard had live
    ammunition in their weapons?  [*read answers*]

    Yes _____   No _____   Uncertain _____

    Didn't consider it _____   Other _____

Q.  What things were not communicated to you during
    this period to your satisfaction?

R.  Would your behavior have been different if you had
    been communicated with more satisfactorily on
    these matters (i.e., curfews, prohibition of
    assembly, live ammunition, etc.)?

    Yes _____   No _____

S.  If yes, in what ways?

T.  Think back to the times you needed such information,
    and suggest how emergency information could have
    reached you quickly.

U.  What methods would you suggest for communicating
    such information to every member of the university
    (i.e., students, faculty, administration, etc.)?

IV. Internal Communication

    A.  [For non-students only]  What problems have you
        *personally experienced* in communicating (talking
        and listening, sending and receiving messages) with
        people and offices within the university?

        1.  Upward (people in a position superior to your
            own)

        2.  Horizontal (people on the relatively same level
            with you)

        3.  Downward

B.  What solutions or recommendations do you see for
    these problems?

    1.  Upward

    2.  Horizontal

    3.  Downward

C.  What offices and persons have you found to be
    available and receptive to you?

D.  What problems of communication do you see when you
    stand back and look at the university in its
    entirety?

    1.  Upward

    2.  Horizontal

    3.  Downward

    4.  External communication

E.  What solutions or recommendations do you see for
    these problems?

    1.  Upward

    2.  Horizontal

    3.  Downwards

    4.  External Communication

F.  [For students only]  What problems have you *personally
    experienced* in communicating (talking and listening,
    sending and receiving) with people and offices with-
    in the university?

G.  Have you had any difficulties in communicating with

    1.  Advisors

    2.  Instructors

    3.  Department or school

    4.  College

    5.  Student Affairs Offices

    6.  Student government

    7.  Business and Finance Offices

    8.  Which of the above have you tried to contact?

H.  What solutions or recommendations do you see for these problems?

I.  What offices and persons have you found to be available and receptive to you?

V.  Internal Credibility

    A.  Please list the three most credible or believable sources (people or offices) within the university.

    B.  Please list the three least credible or believable sources (people or offices) within the university.

VI.  Official Channels of Communication

    A.  What people or offices have been designated by the university to resolve such problems as [probe for specifics and the hierarchy]

        1.  Unfair grades

        2.  Poor advising

        3.  Parking and traffic problems

        4.  Academic rules and regulations

        5.  Social rules and regulations

    B.  What are the main divisions (i.e., those headed by Vice Presidents) of the university?  [Get names of Veeps]

    C.  As you think back over the interview, are there any of your answers you would like to expand? Are there any other problems our questions didn't explore?

Name of Interviewer

Date of Interview

Duration of Interview

Mode of interview (telephone vs face-to-face)

APPENDIX C

RECOMMENDATIONS FROM THE TASK FORCE ON COMMUNICATION

June 15, 1970

TO:   University Commission to Implement a Commitment to
      Non-Violence

FROM:   Task Force on Communication

The events of early May demonstrated the interdependence
of the university and the community.  The evidence suggests
that the communication interfaces between the City of Kent
and Kent State University were inadequate, particularly at
moments of crisis.  We feel that the university will have to
assume responsibility for initiating the actions necessary
for improving this situation.

Therefore, we recommend to President White that he
immediately appoint a liaison executive from his office to
represent him with city officials.  Such an individual should
either be empowered to speak for the President or have immediate access to him (or his designate during times of the
President's absence from the city).  His major responsibilities would be:  (1) to maintain regular face-to-face communication with the Mayor and other city officials, developing
personal relationships and orienting them on such topics as
the goals, structures and functions of KSU; (2) to place
himself in close propinquity to the Mayor during all periods
of crisis and impending crisis.

August 13, 1970

TO:    University Commission to Implement a Commitment to
       Non-Violence

FROM:  Task Force on Communication

                 Emergency Recommendations

1.  *Poor Upward Communication*.   The research on this variable
    clearly indicates that managers of any organization must
    *actively seek* upward-directed communication.  "Good news
    travels up, bad news down."  Valid decision making in
    any situation obviously requires knowledge of the bad
    news--information about the problems.  The administration
    must demonstrate that it wishes to listen especially to
    bad news, must demonstrate that it seeks to know the
    problems of all members of the KSU community.  Then it
    must use its authority to bring about student and faculty
    participation in decisions at all levels.  But mere par-
    ticipation is not enough.  There is considerable evidence
    to suggest that there is too much reliance at KSU on the
    formal advisory system (made up, in the eyes of many, of
    only the "good guys").  Ad hoc groups must also be heard.
    Often the ad hoc groups feel most deeply about issues,
    and are potential sources of information about dissent
    and confrontations.  Too often these groups are ignored;
    in some cases discredited.

        Two Vice Presidents revealed in interviews their
    isolation from faculty and students.  It was also revealed
    that it is now much more difficult to gather "intelligence"
    about student dissidents than it had been "a year ago."
    Part of this problem could be attributed to the driving

underground of radical groups, and as one Dean observed, from "treating dissenters as the enemy."

In summary, the administration (an all levels of authority within the university) must actively seek upward-directed communication. It must tap the informal systems of students and faculty. It must listen.

2. *Inadequate Planning of Emergency Systems*. From the very beginning of our data-gathering we have shared findings and recommendations with those who will be responsible for communication in future crises. Some of the suggestions below have been accepted; some have already been acted upon.

The key word in establishing such systems is *redundancy*. All of the available media must be employed if we hope to reach a majority of the university community. There must be back-up systems in case of overloads, breakdowns or sabotage. For example, on the morning of May 4, at least three buildings received bomb threats. (In some cases they were never given an "all-clear.") Telephone calls made by persons outside the chain-of-authority with unfamiliar voices were challenged in some cases (e.g., unknown voices calling to order cancellation of classes were challenged.) And, as is well known, the breakdown of the telephone system on the afternoon of May the fourth contributed further to anxiety and confusion. Redundancy and back-up systems must be established.

In addition, there must be a *willingness to communicate during* times of emergency. Visibility may be the catchword of the day, but during times of grave danger

and confusion, the members of the university community
need to know the facts, pleasant or unpleasant, and the
position of the authority figure(s), pleasant or unpleasant, if for no other reason that to be reassured
that *someone* is in charge.

A.  Access to the Operations Center to be coordinated by
    the Executive Assistant to the President for Emergency
    Operations (John Huffman) should be granted at least
    to the President, Vice Presidents, Presidents of the
    Faculty Senate and the Student Body, and the
    Coordinator of Internal Communication (or their
    designates).

        It is imperative that Vice President and Provost
    or his designate be intimately informed about the
    emergency.  He must be prepared to reach the academic
    deans--either at home or office--by telephone.  The
    deans must be prepared to do the same with their
    chairmen.  The university cannot fail to keep the
    faculty informed and advised.

B.  During times of crisis or impending crisis, it is
    imperative that the President or his designate speak
    to the university community via electronic media.
    The symbolic importance of the President's face and
    voice during these periods cannot be overemphasized.
    WKSU radio and TV can increase their effectiveness and
    the administration's visibility by several inexpensive
    modifications.  These include:

    1.  The installation of a manual override system for
        WKSU-TV.  Five to eight hours of labor and

approximately $150 in equipment will make it
possible to override all channels of all television sets on campus with emergency audio and
visual signals from Channel 2.   The manual override can be accomplished in five minutes, plus
or minus two.   We strongly recommend that President White authorize such modifications immediately.

2.   The installation of AM amplifiers in all buildings
on campus.   This would permit the reception of
WKSU-*AM* during crisis.   (WKSU-FM can be received
on any FM radio.)   With a transmitter in a
building, WKSU-AM can be received by both electric
and battery operated radios.   In addition, transmission extends approximately 100-200 feet
(radius) from the building (transmitter).   Therefore, with transmitters in each of the buildings
on campus (they are already in the dorms) battery
operated radios could pick up the WKSU-AM signal
in most areas on the campus--indoors or out.

3.   A public address system for the Commons area
could be connected to WKSU-AM lines (once established in the administration building as suggested
in B.2., above); this would be controlled from
the President's Office, or Operations Center,
for an estimated cost of $200.

4.   A radio transmission system connected to WKSU
could be established in President White's office,
or Operations Center so that broadcasts could be
beamed directly to the radio station and

distributed immediately for an estimated cost of
$400.  (Telephones may be used without additional
equipment, but the quality of reproduction is
poor.)

5.  We propose the following systems only as possibilities to be considered:

a.  A transmission system connected to WKSU-TV
could also be set up in President White's
office or in any other desired location.  A
permanent system could be established for
approximately $85,000.  Such a system could
be used as a regular information system as
well as in a crisis situation; thus allowing
greater visibility for the President.  Regular
use of this system would insure greater
functional reliability than if the system
were used only during crisis periods.  The
quality of this system would allow commercial
stations to use the tapes.

b.  A minimal crisis broadcast system could be
set up for approximately $25,000.  Such a
system has the disadvantage of a poor quality
picture, not unlike that of a bank security
system.  Such a picture quality would not be
picked up by commercial TV stations.

c.  Both of these above systems can be made
portable.  A portable minimal broadcast system with vehicle included would cost approximately $30,000.  A portable TV transmission

system of good quality with microwave equipment and vehicle would run approximately
$120,000.  Such a system could be used any-
where on the campus at any time on a regular
as well as crisis basis.

C.  Other media and systems should be established.  These
include:

1.  The purchase of at least one and perhaps several
sound trucks which can traverse all areas of the
campus.  Such vehicles can broadcast messages
and suggest that listeners tune in to other
sources of official information such as WKSU
radio and TV.

2.  The establishing of an emergency telephone system
which would remain operative even if Ohio Bell
finds it necessary to reduce service because of
overloads.  These telephones should include those
of the top administration, the person in charge
of each dorm, all academic deans, all department
chairmen, all school directors and heads of all
instructional units (e.g., the University School);
it should also include the heads of all vital
services (such as health, security, maintenance
and transportation).  At least one telephone in
each building on campus should be so designated
if it does not include one of the offices listed
above.  The list of numbers should be revised
monthly by the Executive Assistant for Emergency
Operations.

3.  All academic and administrative officers should
    have the home and office phone numbers of all
    members of his department available to him at
    office and home. Departments should be reminded
    by their deans to establish an emergency tele-
    phone system. (This has not yet been established
    in many departments.)

4.  Paper, address labels, etc., should be provided
    by the Internal Communication Coordinator in
    printing shops both on and off the campus. (An
    *FYI* explaining the events of May 1 to May 3 was
    rolling off the press on Monday, May 4, but it
    could not be distributed once the campus was
    closed.)

5.  Leaflets should be distributed to all dormitories
    (under room doors rather than in mail boxes),
    posted on all doors of academic buildings, and
    be distributed to large off-campus housing units
    (e.g., College Towers and Glenmorris).

6.  A large team of messengers must be available in
    case of total telephone failure (as happened
    during the last crisis). A telephone directive
    can be challenged during a crisis. The messengers
    could also be used in distributing leaflets as
    prescribed above.

7.  A cooperative emergency radio system must be
    established. Agreement should be sought from
    commercial radio stations to break into regular
    programming to read verbatim all official

announcements from the university administration during an emergency or incipient emergency. Partial data reveal that the stations "most listened to" by KSU students and faculty (including that difficult-to-reach group of commuters) are WKSU, WKNT, WHBC, WGAR, WHLO, WKYC and WAKR.

8. The Coordinator of Internal Communication should be designated as the liaison between the Operations Center and the University News Service, thus guaranteeing the authenticity of all official releases to the emergency radio system and other mass media.

9. The Coordinator of Internal Communication should be authorized to expand Newsrap (4000) to 5 lines and the Information Service (3000) to 10 lines.

10. Whenever possible, the "Saturation System" approved by the UCICNV for communicating security changes should be employed, particularly when the lead time is available to announce faculty meetings, encourage classroom discussion, etc.

11. The "Saturation System" should also be employed before fall quarter to communicate the location of campus television sets, the dial numbers of WKSU-AM and FM, and the telephone numbers of Newsrap (4000) and the Information Center (3000) and the Rumor Control Center.

12. We urge Mr. Huffman to try a "dry run" of his procedures some time before fall quarter, scrubbing the mission only at the point of releasing

emergency information.  This should provide him
with insight into the amount of time needed to
assemble his group in the Operations Center and
in alerting participants (such as WKSU radio and
TV, Internal Communication, etc.)

D.  It would be unwise to specify in great detail the
input systems into the Operations Center, but it is
obvious that radio and telephone communication be
available between the Center and Campus Police, City
Police, WKSU radio and TV, etc.

We repeat our previous recommendation (June 15,
1970) that the President take all necessary initiative
to "appoint a liaison executive from his office to
represent him with city officials.  Such an individual
should either be empowered to speak for the President
or have immediate access to him (or his designate
during times of the President's absence from the
city).  His major responsibilities would be:  (1) to
maintain regular face-to-face communication with the
Mayor and other city officials, developing personal
relationships and orienting them on such topics as
the goals, structures and functions of KSU; (2) to
place himself in close propinquity to the Mayor during
all periods of crisis and impending crisis."

3.  *Ambiguous Authority Structure.*  The recent appointment of
Mr. John Huffman to the position of Executive Assistant
to the President for Emergency Operations was a splendid
opportunity to clarify the confusion about emergency-
chains-of-authority.  If anything, however, it compounded

the confusion. "Will he *coordinate* or will he make the decisions?" asked many interviewees since the appointment. These issues may have been recently resolved, but if so they have not been communicated. The confusion remains. Therefore, we recommend strongly and urgently that the President reconsider and announce the chain-of-authority operative in his absence. If he wishes to delegate full authority to others during various kinds of emergencies, these chains-of-authority should also be communicated fully, and whether they apply during his presence as well as his absence.

We recommend that specialized chains-of-authority be activated only by the President or his designate after considering all available information. (To decide otherwise could lead to a scramble for authority as individuals interpret emergencies in different ways.)

Finally, we acknowledge the President's prerogative in these matters, that he may choose to ignore these recommendations, but in any case we implore him to make clear whatever arrangements he selects *in order that all know where to look for guidance in an emergency.*

4.  *"Bad Luck" Factors.* Try to anticipate as suggested above, specific contingencies, and if these fail--Punt!

September 2, 1970

TO:   University Commission to Implement a Commitment to
      Non-Violence

FROM:   Task Force on Communication

## Recommendations

1.  It is imperative in the weeks and months ahead that
    President White maintain maximum exposure, in person and
    via the electronic media outlined in our previous report,
    with all members of the KSU community.

2.  No less than one academic dean (to be selected annually
    by his peers) should participate in cabinet meetings and
    be requested to specify at least two items for the weekly
    agendum.

3.  The President is requested to delegate increased authority
    to his Vice Presidents in order to free him for symbolic
    and substantive, face-to-face communication.  (We hesitate
    to recommend the appointment of an Executive Vice-President
    because of the dangers of creating *an additional layer*
    between the President and his internal constituents.)

4.  The President should establish an "Academic Cabinet," to
    meet monthly, for the purpose of keeping his office in-
    formed of the problems of the academic sector.  The member
    ship should include the academic deans and the Presidents
    of Graduate Student Council and Student Body.

5.  We recommend that the Provost establish an Academic Sub-
    Cabinet, to include the Provost, all deans (should they
    continue to exist), all department chairmen and fifteen
    students chosen at large by their peers.

6.  The President--and the Vice-Presidents--are encouraged to

participate in systematic, *informal*, meetings with all academic departments, dorms and major service offices within the university during the next academic year.

7.  We recommend the abolition of colleges.  This must be accompanied, of course, by curricular antonomy within the instructional units (departments and schools) and *close budgetary controls*, combined with an expanded staff in the office of the Provost (unemployed KSU deans should be given the first consideration).  Our desire is to flatten the soaring pyramid as well as to give departments-- our only hope to provide personalization and group identification to the student--the opportunity to innovate. (The mathematical rule for limits of span-of-control are irrelevant in this case because the academic departments have proved their exclusion from the principle by virtue of their *lack of interdependence*.)

8.  *Full consideration* should be given to the proposal to have the academic sector absorb the personnel and functions of the Student Affairs Division.

9.  All non-academic divisions should be repeatedly reminded that their sole function, their sole reason for existence, is to facilitate teaching and learning; that "students are the only customers we have."

10.  The Faculty Senate is encouraged to request permanently the attendance of the Vice President for Student Affairs (should the position continue to exist) in the interest of improved horizontal communication.

11.  Student Affairs Counselors should be placed in every department of the university (regardless of the decision

on Recommendation No. Eight, above).  His function will
be to advise faculty and students alike on the methods
of acquiring student services.  Hopefully, it will encourage the self-sufficiency of the department (as well as
provide academic feedback to those responsible for
coordinating student services).  Should the collegial
structure continue to exist, we recommend that such
counselors also be attached to each college office.

12.  To "tie together" all elements of the university we
recommend the immediate constitution of a University
Senate, comprising administration, faculty, students,
staff and citizens of Kent, Ohio as the highest policy-
making body within KSU.  (We should encourage, in turn,
the franchising and representation of the KSU community
in city policy-making).

13.  We recommend that all *departments* improve academic
advising by:

A.  Abandoning the assumption that all faculty members
are willing and able to provide academic advising.

B.  That volunteers be identified--with the understanding
that excellence in advising will be adequately
rewarded, subject to student evaluation.

C.  That an Advising Coordinator be established who will
maintain central records on all advisees, keep up-
to-date with all changes, keep all advisors so informe
and encourage full communication between the departmental Student Affairs Counselor, students and faculty

14.  Each academic department should select from its faculty,
by vote of student majors, a departmental Ombudsman (with

the understanding that students may appeal to an Academic
Ombudsman located in the Provost's office).

15. Departments are strongly encouraged to sub-divide all
    classes with an enrollment exceeding fifty students--even
    at the expense of cutbacks in graduate programs.  The sole
    exception to this should be to maximize the exposure of
    proven, demonstrably effective and respected professors.

16. We recommend that all offices of the university provide
    an intensive orientation for *all new employees* (to be
    supported by the appropriate divisions, but with partici-
    pation by all other divisions), effective by the fall of
    1972.

17. Finally, we recommend that all departments move immediately
    to include a significant percentage of faculty (if not
    otherwise included) and students in basic departmental
    policy-making.

APPENDIX D

PHOTOGRAPHS BY JOHN P. FILO

COPYRIGHT 1970 Tarentum, Pa. Valley Daily News — Photographed by John P. Filo